LAND OF THE MORNING

*A Civilian Internee's Poignant Memories
of Sunshine and Shadows*

Jean McAnlis McMurdie

RED APPLE PUBLISHING

Copyright © 2001 Jean McAnlis McMurdie
Laguna Woods, California

FIRST EDITION
Second Printing

RED APPLE
PUBLISHING
15010 113th St. KPN
Gig Harbor, WA 98329-5014
(253) 884-1450

Printed by Gorham Printing
Rochester, WA 98579

ISBN 1-880222-43-4

Library of Congress Control Number 2001132092

Cover design by Kathryn E. Campbell

Photo of Mt. Mayon, Legaspi, Albay, Philippines
Hand-painted Christmas card by the Franciscan Nurses,
December 1944

Disclaimer: Although the author and publisher have tried to
ensure accuracy and completeness of the events, they assume
no responsibility for errors, inaccuracies, omissions, or any
inconsistencies. Events are colored by the author's viewpoint
and how they affected her.

DEDICATION

To the memory
of my parents
William Wilbur McAnlis, M.D. and **Josephine Wilson McAnlis**
Stalwart Christian missionaries
beloved by Americans and Filipinos alike,
and, in 1964, made honorary citizens of the province of Albay,
after almost forty years of labor in the Philippines.
Their children rise up and call them blessed!
And, in honor of
all the service men and women who fought in the Pacific,
especially
those members of the 11th **Airborne**
who gave of themselves to rescue us in our extremity!
We will never forget you!

ACKNOWLEDGMENTS

I WROTE THESE MEMOIRS after much urging from my husband, Bill, my children, and many friends who had heard at least part of my story—especially my World War II years.

Thanks to all those who assisted in readying this manuscript for publication. My husband Bill gave verbal encouragement and constructive criticism of style and readability. He even got a few meals when I was deep in writing. My sister Ruth offered several corrections after reading the rough draft—one of which was "Don't give my age!" She also was able to clarify some of my hazy recollections.

Other MK's (missionary kids) who grew up with me and went through the same experiences have also read the first drafts. Among them are George and Bob MacDonald. Bob, a retired high school English teacher, gets the newly minted "Order of the Fine-toothed Comb" award for his meticulous proof reading. George has graciously allowed me to reprint a number of maps he had drawn up for his own presentations. He also caught some errors that had escaped the eagle eyes of other proofreaders. Tom Bousman, a "Manila kid," has read the manuscript and has supplied me with a number of drawings he made while at Los Baños Internment Camp. He has kindly permitted their reproduction in this book.

Other hard-working proofreaders were Sarah Wolf (another recipient of the "Fine-toothed Comb" medal), Lora Morgan, Marie Deroin, Ruth Haney, and David McAnlis. Rev. Ed Bryant and Prof. Sig Lee also proofed and critiqued the manuscript. They offered helpful suggestions for the organization of the text. Peggy Meyer, my editor and publisher, was of inestimable help.

Books I consulted while writing my memoirs include *The Los Baños Raid* by Lt. Gen. E. M. Flannigan, Jr. (Jove Books, 1987) which has recently been re-released under the title *Angels at Dawn, The Los Baños Raid,* and *Deliverance at Los Baños* by Anthony Arthur (St. Martin's Press, 1985). *"We Band of Angels,"* an account of the Army and Navy nurses who worked at Santo Tomas and Los Baños after their capture, renewed memories. It was written by Elizabeth M. Norman and published by Random House in 1999. Other books, which I have read but do not have in my library, were personal memoirs by Carol Terry Talbot and by Grace Nash. I relied heavily on my mother's journal which she kept in various notebooks and blank pages in her Bible (in the archives at the University of Oregon in Eugene).

Pictures, other than the maps and picture of Mayon which George MacDonald supplied, are snapshots which had either been sent "home" to relatives before the war or had survived as undeveloped film through the war until retrieved and developed by Kenneth MacDonald, as mentioned in the manuscript text. These latter pictures show the grainy effects of mildew and mold on the undeveloped film. Sketches and outline drawings are from Tom Bousman. Pictures of both Santo Tomas Internment Camp and Los Baños Internment Camp are from Christmas cards hand drawn by the nursing Sisters and given to my dad and mom on Christmas Day, 1944. Any errors are solely the responsibility of the author.

PREFACE

THE EVENTS IN THIS BOOK are those experienced by the writer and present my memories of childhood on the foreign mission field, teen years as a prisoner of the Japanese during World War II, and a brief summary of the following years as a preacher's wife, registered nurse, mom, teacher, and traveler.

Segments about my war experiences, which appear in quotes and bold type, are from my mother's journal that she kept in various unobtrusive notebooks and even on blank pages of her Bible to keep them from being discovered by our captors. I remember those war years quite well since I was almost thirteen years old when the war started and sixteen when we were rescued. My sister Ruth has refreshed my memories of some events, but where we cannot agree on details, I have gone with my memories. She will have to write her own book!

The text divides into three main parts:

PART ONE highlights the beautiful Islands where I was born and raised, and it introduces you to some of the main characters.

PART TWO, which makes up well over half of this book, tells of our war years—Escape to the Hills; Life in Hiding; Our Capture; Internment; House Arrest; Re-internment; Starvation; Dawn Rescue; Repatriation. In all those years of war we did not doubt our country's concern for our welfare nor our gracious God's loving and protecting hand, no matter the circumstances.

PART THREE covers, in highly condensed form, my years since "The War."

(Please note that the italicized words in poem form are from the *Philippine National Anthem*.)

—JMM

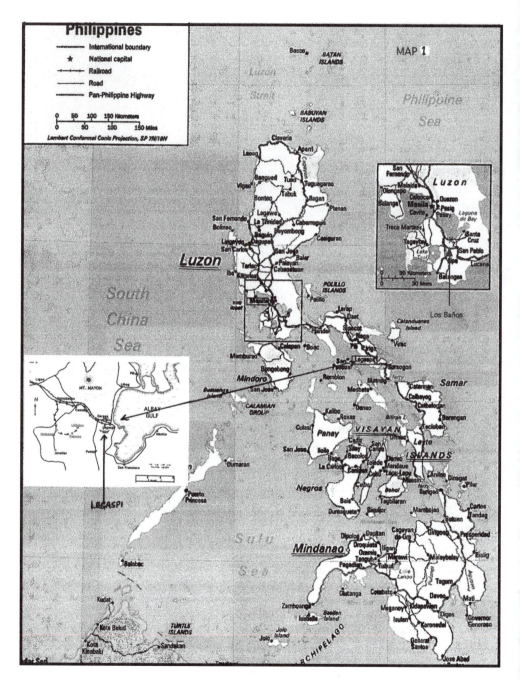

MAP 1

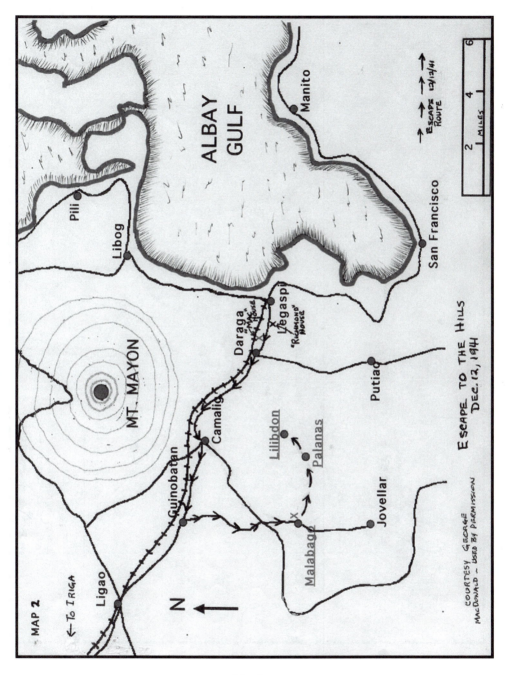

MAP 2

9

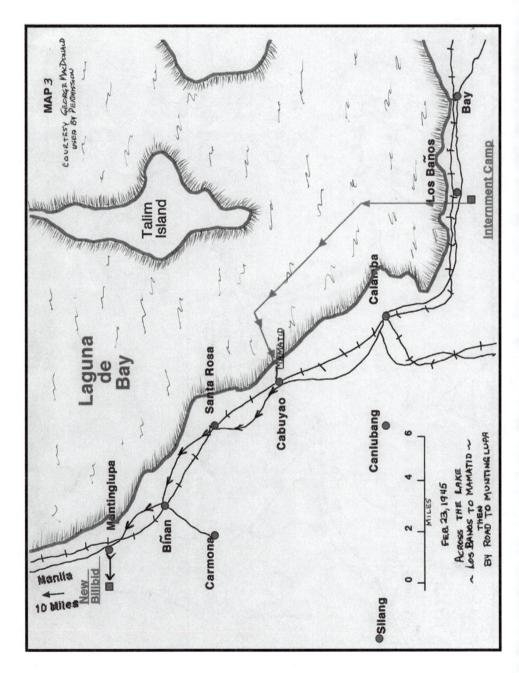

MAP 3

COURTESY GEORGE MACDONALD
USED BY PERMISSION

Talim Island

Laguna de Bay

Bay

Los Baños

Internment Camp

Calamba

MAMATID

Santa Rosa

Cabuyao

Canlubang

Muntinglupa

Biñan

Carmona

Silang

Manila
10 Miles
New Bilibid

FEB. 23, 1945
~ ACROSS THE LAKE ~
LOS BANOS TO MAMATID ~
THEN
BY ROAD TO MUNTINGLUPA

MILES
0   2   4   6

MAP 3

10

CONTENTS

PART THREE

PART ONE

PROLOGUE

Five thirty a.m., December 12, 1941. It is not yet light in this Philippine town just 14 degrees north of the equator, where day and night are each about twelve hours long. My brother Dave and I have been up for ten minutes or so and have noticed a peculiar fluctuating hum of voices from the road about 200 feet from our home. We make a hurried, quiet trip to the kitchen where Feling, our cook, should have been busily preparing breakfast. We find him pacing the floor, wringing his hands. The rest of the house is still. Dad and Mom and our sister Ruth are still asleep. They'll be up around 6:00. We'll all eat breakfast by 6:30, and after morning prayers, we kids will be on our way to school (walking the kilometer or so) and the folks off to work by 7:00.

Feling explains his distress quickly. The Japanese have landed in Legaspi, about one and a half kilometers east of our house. Filipinos are evacuating the area. He wants to take his family and leave too, but he needs to inform his employers first.

Dave and I are in a quandary. One hard and fast rule at our house is that NO ONE bothers the folks until 6:00—EVER! We debate awhile as to whether this news is important enough to bend the rule. About 5:45 we decide that we must take our chances, and so we timidly knock on their bedroom door. Quickly telling them what Feling has told us, we retreat and watch with astonishment as they spring into action.

CHAPTER 1

BEGINNINGS

What was going on? How did we come to be in the Philippines?

For Dave and me and my other brothers and sister, it all goes back to Emporia College in Kansas where Dad and Mother met, courted, and married in 1918 before Dad went off to war. In France and Germany he served as a medic, sometimes even going into "no man's land" to assist the wounded.

While at college, they had both belonged to the Foreign Mission Society and hoped to be accepted and sent to a foreign field when they completed their education. Mother taught high school English for a year, waiting for Dad to come home from war. Dad entered medical school after his army stint and Mother did all sorts of work to help support the family. She even ran a boarding house (meals only for a dozen medical students) for awhile. Two sons, Bill and Allen, were born to them while Dad was in medical training.

Late in 1925 they were sent out by the Presbyterian Board for Foreign Missions. Dad wanted to go to Korea where his younger brother, a dentist, was assigned to the mission hospital at Seoul. Mother was hoping for China. What they got was the Philippines where Dad would "fill in" for a missionary doctor who was on furlough in the States. Later, Dad would be transferred to another mission station in the Islands. I must admit that I'm very glad that the Philippines would become my birthplace.

CHAPTER 2

LAND OF THE MORNING

Land of the morning, Child of the sun returning,
With fervor burning, Thee do our souls adore!
Land dear and holy, Cradle of noble heroes.

*P*opulated mostly by Malaysian and Polynesian peoples, there were also many Chinese. Spaniards, who came in the 1500s also left a remnant, and in following years, a few Japanese had made their homes in the Philippines. Living in some of the mountainous regions were the aboriginal peoples, the Igorots and the Ifugaos, considered to be the original inhabitants. The Nigritos, a pigmy tribe, lived in jungles of the northern part of the Bicol Provinces. There were also some pigmy tribes in Mindanao, the large southern island. They remained unknown to the world until well after WWII.

The Philippines had been a possession of Spain since the 1500s. They were acquired in 1898 by the United States after the Spanish-American War. Filipino patriots had resisted the Spanish, and a number fought on against the American forces for several years around 1900, wanting their independence. High on Filipinos' roster of heroes are Jose Rizal, who was martyred by the Spanish; Apolinario Mabini, who also led resistance to Spain; and Emilio Aguinaldo, who led the fight against American forces under Douglas MacArthur's father, Arthur MacArthur.

Filipinos also lay claim to famous painters such as Armosolo and Ancheta. Vocal and instrumental arts flourished in the Philippines following their liberation from Spain. Filipinos are also gifted orators and actors.

In about 1902 peace came to the Islands—seven thousand and some, arranged in an archipelago stretching more than a 1000 miles over the ocean (see map #1). The main northern island is Luzon. A band of medium-sized islands, called the Visayan Islands, comprise the middle of the archipelago, and Mindanao with the Sulu archipelago make up the southern portion of the country. The Philippines is located south of Taiwan and east of Vietnam. The Pacific Ocean lies to the east, the South China Sea to the west, and the Celebes Sea to the south.

Ever within thy skies and through thy fields,
And o'er thy hills and seas,
Do we behold thy radiance, feel the throb
Of glorious liberty!
Thy Banner, dear to all our hearts,
Its sun and stars alight,
Oh, never shall its shining field
Be dimmed by tyrant's might!
Beautiful land of love, O land of light,
In thine embrace 'tis rapture to lie!

CHAPTER 3

BEAUTIFUL LAND

All of the Philippine archipelago lies in the tropics. Tropical forest, much of it actually jungle, covers vast areas of the land, especially in the hilly or mountainous regions. In the warm, humid weather, trees reach incredible heights and girths. I've hiked trails near Iriga, about fifty miles north of my hometown, where the over-arching trees were festooned with orchids of every color imaginable. Parrots and other multi-colored birds called from the branches. There were ferns and tropical plants in the undergrowth. Delicate waterfalls splashed down rocky cliffs into crystal-clear pools. Waterfall water or rain shower—neither one of them so cold as to shock you.

There were many open areas where farming was common, especially in the provinces north of Manila where the bulk of rice was grown for Philippine consumption. Most lowland rice requires level land which can be shaped into small fields which are then diked to maintain a constant level of water in which rice grows. Corn was the staple crop in the Visayan Islands.

Our Bicol Provinces were very productive of coconuts, though we grew plenty of rice and many vegetables. Coconuts grew everywhere, even on the beaches where the nuts, fallen from other coconut trees and carried by the tides, would wash up on the shore, sprout, and take root in the sand! The Bicol Provinces had many coconut plantations, since copra was our main export crop. Tropical fruit of all kinds grew almost anywhere in the Philippines, except in the very high mountain areas. In the lowlands, we had banana, papaya, some pineapple, mango, guava and many exotic fruits unknown in the U.S. until recently. Coffee and cacao (for chocolate) trees often grew wild.

Other islands specialized in raising sugar cane, although it grew almost anywhere it was planted. The island of Negros (pronounced NEIGH-gross) was an important sugar producer. Yet another island, Mindanao, with a large upland plateau area, concentrated on growing pineapple for export. Dole Company had a large cannery there.

In the high mountainous region north of the central provinces on Luzon was the city of Baguio. It was "vacation land" for foreigners in the Islands and for Filipino business people as well. There it was cool, and even cold at times. Pine trees grew well, and I remember the fragrance of a pine wood fire on a cool Baguio night when our family vacationed there. Strawberries and cabbage and other cool-weather crops did well at that altitude. We did not have the refrigerated trucks or storage facilities then, so we could enjoy these "Stateside" fruits and veggies only when we were in Baguio. I think the folks enjoyed them more than we kids did!

But, there were more than just gustatory treats available to us in the Philippines! Can anyone do justice to describing a sunset over Manila Bay (or anywhere in the Islands, for that matter!)? Even film does not capture all the flaming colors! And, the flowers that bloomed profusely all year long! Too many kinds to enumerate! The gorgeous butterflies and moths that flitted here and there only enhanced the beauty of the countryside. We didn't have four seasons, so green leaves were on the trees and plants all year long, keeping our Islands verdant. Occasional splashes of vari-colored vegetation added variety. Nor can I forget coconut palm fronds glistening in the moonlight as they swayed to and fro in the light trade winds.

Our seas were usually calm, bright blue or turquoise color, and home to multitudes of fish, which were caught and sold on a daily basis, and formed the basic protein for many Filipino diets. Fishermen went out, usually at night with a torch to attract the fish, in small bancas (outrigger canoes, made from hollowed out logs with bamboo outriggers attached). The seas were the byways between islands, and many people traveled by boat, large and small.

In the mountains, engineers and geologists had found precious metals, mostly gold and silver, and mining was a very important industry in the northern provinces of Luzon. Timber was another valuable export from the Philippines, as was also copra, the dried meat of the coconut. Another export was abaca fiber for making hemp ropes. Mt. Mayon, in my province of Albay, was an active volcano. We used to enjoy the hot springs on the lower, eastern slopes, and sometimes picnicked there, hardboiling eggs in the small, bubbling, mineral-water springs. After the war, the vents and springs on the mountain side were utilized to provide geo-thermal power to the entire city of Manila.

There were also poisonous snakes on our Islands, mostly in the rice paddies, though the servants did find a nest of cobras in the dirt-floored garage of one of our Albay mission homes once. Cockroaches and termites had to be battled constantly. And, yes, there were sharks in some waters, but one understood the risk and took adequate precautions. For instance, we could not swim in Legaspi Harbor, since the beach shelved off sharply just a few feet from shore, and the sharks could come up to within a few feet of the beach. But, a few miles up the road was a marvelous swimming beach with a long, shallow, bench underwater to make it safe from sharks.

CHAPTER 4

BEAUTIFUL LAND OF LOVE

---

*T*he people were gentle (for the most part), generous, romantic, humorous, fun-loving, and above all—patriotic! They loved their land and worked hard in it. Many were poor; some were in the middle class; and some very rich. But, it was their country, and they were proud of it. A Filipino folk story, found in all elementary school reading books, tells how when people were first made that God shaped the dough like man-shaped cookies. He burned the first batch, and that was the black race. On the second batch, He was so afraid to over-bake them that He took them out too early—and that, of course, was the white race. The third batch was taken out of the oven a nice golden brown, and that was the Filipinos!

Farmers—men, women and children—tilled the muddy rice fields and planted tender plants, tended the dykes and dams of the water supply. A Filipino folk song went: *"Planting rice is never fun! Bent from morn 'til the set of sun! Cannot stand and cannot sit, Cannot rest for a little bit!"* Then, at harvest time—after the rice paddies had been drained and allowed to dry out—the farmers reaped the golden fields, threshed the grain, and dried it on mats in the hot sun.

City folk—artisans, business and professional people, artists, merchants, government workers, bankers, teachers—worked to help the Philippines grow into their dreams.

The Philippine flag shows a large white triangle with the sun in the middle and three stars at each angle. These represent the three main island groups, all sharing the same sun. At the top of the flag is a blue field, standing for loyalty; at the bottom is a red field, reminding the people of the blood of the martyrs.

At the start of WWII, there were about eighteen million Filipino citizens, speaking at least eighty-seven different dialects throughout the Islands. In 1935 the Philippines had gained commonwealth status under United States' protection. It was at this time that President Manuel Quezon asked retired General Douglas MacArthur to come back to the Philippines (he had served there in the U.S. Army in the 1920s) to accept the position as head of their military. He took up his duties in the Islands in 1936. The Filipinos had already elected a legislative body, elected a president and vice-president, and set up the court system. Now they set about practicing the skills necessary to govern themselves when their country would become a free nation in 1946.

The Roman Catholic church had, of course, been present since Spain claimed the land for King Philip and church at the time of Magellan in 1521. When the Americans came in 1898, many teachers, engineers, missionaries, and business people, as well as military and civil government personnel, came to the Islands. English became the universal language. All school classes, elementary through graduate school, used English-language texts. American educators headed up the high schools and normal schools. There were many private academies as well as private universities, some of which—for instance, Santo Tomas University—predated Harvard and Yale Universities. Various denominations also established Bible Schools and regular universities as well as Theological Seminaries for Filipino nationals.

Some of the Protestant missions had set up a system of "comity," which essentially divided up areas of the Islands for exclusive work by any one denomination. Every Mission Board, Protestant and Catholic, had a headquarters compound in Manila, with a chairman of the mission, a treasurer, and any other mission official needed to direct the overall work of that particular mission. Also, on the compound might be a training school for lay-workers and a seminary. There might even be a church building associated with a seminary where the students could get in their practice. The congregation would be made up of local residents who belonged to that particular denomination, Filipinos and foreigners. Most of us kids hated to go to Manila, since it was crowded and hot and there was little for a kid to do while the folks took care of business.

24

CHAPTER 5

OUR FAMILY ARRIVES IN THE PHILIPPINES

*I*n late 1925 or early 1926, when Dad and Mother, with Bill and Allen, arrived in the Islands, they spent more than a year at Silliman University Hospital in Dumaguete, Negros Oriental Province. Dad filled in as medical director of the hospital while Dr. Cunningham and his family were on furlough.

There my sister Ruth was born shortly before Dad and Mother were transferred to Albay (pronounced AHL-buy) Province. Ruth got to visit Mindanao and the Visayan Islands when she was about fourteen, and I was scheduled to have my turn at "the tour" in 1942. Alas, it was not to be!

Dad was assigned to open a new hospital in Legaspi, Albay, on the island of Luzon. Legaspi is about 350 kilometers (215 miles) southeast of Manila. I was born there in 1929, and brother David came along in 1931. The mission station in Legaspi, Albay Province, had been there for over twenty years when Dad and Mom came.

Our station in Albay Province was on the Pacific Ocean side of the island, and we had trade winds to moderate our climate. (Manila, by contrast, was situated on the hot lee side of Luzon, on beautiful Manila Bay, whose entrance is guarded by Corregidor.) Beautiful Mt. Mayon (pronounced "my-OWN"), an active volcano, often displaying a red tip at night, rose to a height of about

25

3000 meters (over 8000 feet) not many kilometers from our home. There were other volcanic cones, all dormant, in the provinces that made up the Bicol Peninsula, but none so high or impressive.

Photo of Mt. Mayon, Legaspi, Albay, Philippines

CHAPTER 6

MEMORIES, MEMORIES!

When I was a child, we had one paved road that touched most of the main cities and stretched most of the way from the province of Sorsogon, at the tip of our peninsula, north and west to the province of Camarines Norte. Other roads were of packed dirt (mud, during the rainy season) or gravel, and the traffic was slow and easy. One of my favorite memories is that of a bunch of us mission kids riding on the luggage rack at the back of our 1923 Dodge, feet dangling in the dust while Dad or Vicente drove at the sedate pace of three or four miles per hour.

The railroad started in Legaspi, Albay Province, and ran to Camarines Norte Province where we had to transfer to a ferry to take us across a gulf to another section of Luzon where the railroad picked up again and ran north to Manila. Rail travel was inconvenient and slow, to say the least. We had to carry our own food for the trip. We started in the morning and rode most of the day. The day train had a central aisle with slat benches, in pairs facing each other, down each side. The windows were open (no air conditioning then) and cinders would often get into the unwary eye. At every stop, food vendors would display wondrous delicacies of all sorts, which we kids were never allowed to sample. Late in the afternoon we reached the end of the line for that train. We would off-load, get on a ferry with all our belongings, and travel across the water for an hour or two.

On the other side of the gulf, we would reverse the process, debarking from the ferry and getting on the night train. This train had long benches, in pairs

27

facing each other but sticking out perpendicular to one side of the car. The aisle went down the other side of the car instead of down the middle as common in the States, and people were constantly moving to and fro. Also, there would probably be live chickens and goats or pigs (all in gunny sacks) under some of the benches. The benches were made of slats and were long enough to allow you to stretch out. The benches had a pull-out section which filled the space between the benches. We (probably a maid, not ourselves) would pull out these sections, unroll our mats on the hard "bed" and try to sleep. Since the distance from that point to Manila was not so far, the train would sit at the station until about 11:00 p.m. and then move slowly north, arriving in Manila early in the morning. I personally hated the trip to Manila and remember only a few trips in my entire thirteen years prior to 1942—once to a dentist for an abscessed tooth, once to get my eyeglasses, and another time on our way to vacation in Baguio. Those were enough for this country girl!

The train passed through Daraga, which was just a couple of miles north of our house, on its way to or from Legaspi. It was always fun, when meeting visitors to our mission station, to get to Daraga early, long before the engine could be heard, much less seen. We'd put our ears to the track to "feel" the train coming and then carefully lay a centavo (worth 1/2 cent at that time) on the track so that the train could run over it. Mom and Dad always made sure we were well back from the tracks before the train chugged into the station. Life was slow and easy, and entertainment was where you could find it!

We had a '23 Dodge when I was very little, but I believe we had a later model of some sort after 1936—a big, straight-eight, Studebaker, four-door sedan, I'm told. It was nowhere near as fascinating as the Dodge, which had that lovely luggage rack and detachable isinglass curtains for when it rained. It took quite a bit of doing to get the curtains in place, and the person putting them on usually was drenched with sweat or with rain before the job was done. Of course, if the "windows" were put on, then the interior of the car became so hot that you perspired so heavily that you might as well have left the curtains off and enjoyed the rain!

Tropical rain has to be seen to be believed. We had a saying in our province that during the rainy season it rained all the time, and during the dry season, it rained at least once a day. Sometimes there were only showers, but normal rain came straight down in sheets. During typhoons, these sheets of rain came at you horizontally. But, it was usually warm rain, never chilly except in an occasional typhoon. Rain on a thatch roof also has a more gentle sound than that on a tin roof.

You could actually see the rain advancing over the distant hills. It had such a sharp delineation that more than once I have seen it rain on one side of the road while the other side, less than forty feet away, was perfectly dry. In fact, as the curtain of rain moved toward you, you could gauge pretty well when it was going to arrive, and make your plans accordingly. When I was walking home from school in the afternoons, it was easy to figure out that when I reached the local tienda (small store) selling fresh hot baduya (banana fritters) the rain would be upon me. Of course, I would just have to stop under the overhanging roof to keep dry until the shower passed over. Eating fresh baduya always helped to pass the time. Ruth usually walked faster and made it to the cooked fresh sweet corn stall farther down the road. She was really partial to corn.

CHAPTER 7

GETTING AROUND

---

*T*he majority of Filipinos either walked or took the bus, which ran fairly frequently locally. It also ran at regular intervals to cities and towns north and south of us. We mission kids (MK's) usually walked, or biked (if we had one), or took the bus. All you had to do to catch a ride was to stand at the side of the road and wave your arm as the bus approached. The seats were benches that ran from one side to the other—open on either side. You climbed on wherever there was space. A "conductor" shinnied back and forth on the left running board, hanging on for dear life to the uprights at the end of each bench, and collecting fares. But, I remember a few times when I passed my fare money up to the driver via the other passengers. Getting off where you wanted to required yelling "*Para*" (Stop) or using a very loud "s-s-s-s-st!"—or both in conjunction. The passengers always got a kick out of hearing a white person yelling out. The conductor had a whistle to signal the driver: 1 was *stop*; 2 was *go*; 3 was *back up*! The bus company, ALATCO, was privately owned, and there were two American couples running the business end at the headquarters in Iriga, about 50 kilometers from Legaspi.

One of the ALATCO couples had two children. The eldest, a girl named Patsy, was about my age, and every once in awhile I would be invited to come up to Iriga for several days to visit and play with Patsy. Mother would take me out to the road to catch the Iriga bus, and the driver would make room for me to sit right beside him. He would promise to deliver me safely to the James home, and off we would go. The James's lifestyle was quite different from that of mission families, and Patsy and I never ran out of games to play.

Once "Uncle Jimmy" took his whole family and me to their beach house in Camarines Sur, the next province north. They had a rambling home back from the beach, which was reached via a trail through a coconut grove. The beach was very wide and, wonder of wonders, made of white sand—the first I had ever seen. We had only black sand in my province. At low tide the cook/houseboy would rake up little clams from a cove, using a common garden rake. He made wonderful chowder.

At the market, James's cook also found the sweetest pineapples I've ever tasted. They were miniature size, though fully mature. The way he prepared them for us was to leave on a four- to five-inch segment of stem. Then he would pare the pineapple all around to remove the "eyes" and present them to us when we were sitting out on the lawn in the afternoon. Being outside was important because we ate them just as you would a Popsicle, holding the stem and eating around the pared fruit, which was about the size of a large baking potato. They were very juicy, and messy to eat, but so good.

Our own family outings to local rivers and beaches, usually in company with another missionary family, were always in the car, though we had to hike into the swimming holes in the river. Mother didn't drive, so Vicente would drive the car if Dad was tied up with work at the hospital. Vicente was a jack-of-all-trades who helped at Milwaukee Hospital (named for the Milwaukee area churches which endowed the mission hospital) or wherever he was needed. (Later, on December 12, 1941, he took the car and the old Dodge and hid them deep in an abaca plantation out in the country. It's my understanding that Vicente continued to use the Dodge for years after the war.)

Another time the car was used was when a U.S. Army plane would fly in to our local airstrip. The mission families always vied for hosting the pilots, and whichever car made it out to the field earliest had first dibs. One time a plane came in too far, nosed-up, and flipped in the mud at the end of the strip. The plane was wrecked, and pieces of it were given to each missionary family. The MacDonalds got a big star from the wing, and Uncle Mac mounted it on the ceiling of their sleeping porch. That pilot had to stay even longer since another plane would have to be flown in, and that was fun since he told such wild stories! The folks enjoyed visiting with the pilots too. American visitors were infrequent in the provinces.

CHAPTER 8
OUR "EXTENDED FAMILY"

*T*he problem of how to address our missionary elders when we were kids was solved by referring to them as "Uncle" or "Aunt" in most cases. Occasionally, we used the title "Mr." or "Mrs." We never called them by their first names. That was considered most impolite, and perhaps even impudent. So, my references to Uncle and Aunt will be to those honorary "relatives." Adult Filipinos were always addressed by their title and last name.

Mission "Family"—Albay Station, 1935.
MacDonald family, Smith family, McAnlis family, LaPortes

When I was a little girl, our mission station had four resident missionaries and their wives and children. There were the MacDonalds, the Smiths, the McAnlises (us) and the LaPortes. There was also a single-lady missionary stationed in Sorsogon, the province just south of ours. Until 1934 there were six MacDonald children, three Smith children, and us five McAnlis children. The eldest MacDonald girl, Janet, was sent back to the States for college in 1934. Then, as the years passed, the older kids would be sent back to the States as they grew old enough. The LaPortes never had any children.

Our mission station from the time I was ten years old included the MacDonalds, the LaPortes, and us (the McAnlises) with Miss Rhorbaugh being stationed in the next province south of us. The Smiths had been transferred to work in Manila while we were on furlough in 1938–39. After the Smiths left, the LaPortes moved from the Christian Center apartment into the "Smith" house. In December of 1941 there were only six mission kids left on the station—the youngest three MacDonalds and the youngest three in our family. Bob MacDonald had been sent to Manila to live with the Smiths while he went to high school. His folks wanted him to have the opportunity to study violin with Grace Nash, a concert violinist with the Manila Symphony Orchestra.

Helen MacDonald was a few months older than my sister Ruth; John MacDonald was a few months older than I; and George MacDonald was a few months older than my brother David. Ruth and Helen played together a lot, but John was "a boy!" and he and I pretty much went our separate ways. Besides, he was a year ahead of me in school. George and David played well together, but more commonly it was John and George at their home and David and I at ours.

As for the adults in the mission "family" in pre-war Albay station, Uncle Mac (MacDonald) was senior missionary. He had a hand in almost everything, from planning and constructing the mission buildings to running the print shop that was used to turn out Christian material for use by the Filipinos, or preaching a sermon in Bicol dialect. He was always busy, and whistled tunelessly under his breath as he concentrated. His very WORST word was "peanuts!" Look out when he let loose with that, for it meant he was really exasperated. He typed like a whirlwind, using just his two index fingers. His passion was taking pictures. Sometimes he took movies, which he would run backwards at times, much to our delight! But, movie film was very expensive, so mostly he took stills—lots of them! He almost always had a camera of some sort with him on every occasion. Auntie Margaret, his wife, was almost always in a good humor, and she had the most infectious laugh I have ever heard. It seemed to bubble up from her inmost parts, until it burst out in a hearty laugh. Anyone who was in her presence when she laughed couldn't help but join in the hilarity! Uncle Mac was a firm believer in the efficacy of cod liver oil, but it was Auntie Margaret who spooned it out daily to each child, also those not her own who happened to be staying overnight! She taught all us kids our piano lessons.

The Smiths were a different kind of couple. They had three boys, all at least five years or more older than I was. Uncle Smith (his given name was Stephen, but we always used his last name) was a tall, slim, very pleasant man with an engaging personality. (When I was quite little I used to cling to his long legs, and had a number of reprimands from Mother.) He was theologically trained, and while at Albay station he also preached in dialect as well as English. His specialty, as far as we kids were concerned, were the stories he made up "out of whole cloth." They were about the adventures of Jack, Bill, and Pete—sometimes scary, sometimes just plain exciting, and always ended in a "to be continued" mode! Auntie Smith taught music at the Bible School. She was a soprano, with lots of tremolo in her voice. I remember that she insisted her boys always wear shoes (Keds) when the rest of us were running around barefoot. She never could understand how her kids could get hookworm (which enters the body through the feet) more often than did the rest of us whose feet were toughened. We never snitched on them, but the minute they were out of sight of their mom, those shoes came off. Their feet were much more tender than ours, and easily penetrated by those nasty critters—the hookworms.

The other missionary couple at our station was the LaPortes. We never called them Aunt or Uncle. Dr. LaPorte was in charge of the Christian Center and conducted English service every Sunday evening. He was slightly built, but taller than average. His wife, Margaret, was known throughout the entire area for always tucking a clean white hankie into the band of her wristwatch. Before the war, I never saw her without it. She was always daintily dressed and never looked hot and bothered! And, we never called her anything but Mrs. LaPorte.

Aunt Olive (Rhorbaugh) lived and worked in Sorsogon Province, and we did not have too much to do with her. Good hearted, but tending to be bossy at times, she had many faithful Filipino co-workers.

CHAPTER 9

AND, MY FOLKS

$\mathscr{M}$y folks were Uncle Doc and Aunt Jo to the other mission kids. (The grown-ups called each other by their given names.) Mother's given name was Josephine Osborne, so I guess her shortened name could have been from her first name or from the initials. Dad was about 5 feet 8 inches or so, and he was slightly built, never weighing more than 140 pounds. He and his brother, Albert, were the only two remaining members of the McAnlis clan from Clay Center, Kansas. All their family had died prior to Dad's and Mother's marriage. Dad had light blue eyes that could get a steely look in them if you were out of line. (I never really liked blue eyes.) He had a dry wit and Scottish sense of humor, but as a child I never could quite figure out if he was joking or not. He was strict, but fair; loving but rigorous in maintaining discipline. He was an excellent physician and surgeon, and he enjoyed a very high reputation in the province. He did much community outreach work, setting up traveling clinics staffed by Milwaukee Hospital doctors and nurses. The fluoroscope he brought to the hospital in 1939 was the first in the province and was in use constantly to screen the population for tuberculosis, which was a scourge in our area. He and his staff also volunteered at the local leprosarium.

Dad never stopped teaching. He recruited young doctors from the university medical school in Manila, and gave them what was essentially "residency training." He evidently noted my interest in nursing early on, and when I was eleven years old or so, he permitted me, with the consent of the patient, obviously, to observe surgery when he was operating on one of my friends or classmates. He would discuss the anatomy involved as he went. I remember one operation, osteomyelitis of the left tibia, on a classmate of mine. He started at about 10 a.m. and was still patiently chipping away at the infected area some two hours later when I decided to head home for noon dinner. I told the nurse that I was going, but I didn't interrupt him since he was concentrating. That evening he kidded me about getting "queasy" and having to leave the O.R. He was amused when I told him I just plain got hungry.

Dad's concentration was legendary. He was especially insistent on absolute quiet when he was engaged in a chess match! We could watch but NEVER kibitz! And, he really preferred it if we were entirely out of the room. I think chess was not a game to him. But, he could let down his hair at times too. He always enjoyed the skits that "spoofed" him at our church get-togethers. And, he was very affectionate toward Mother—frequently reaching out to give her a pat on her bottom as she passed, at which she would pretend exasperation! We kids knew better!

I always called my mother just that—Mother. She once told me that her mother, my Grandma Wilson, had been to a circus where the elephant was named Mom, so she never wanted to be called that! Mother was large boned, a little taller than Dad, and outweighed him as well. She was always pleasant to be around and completely practical in her actions—not much nonsense about her but very loving and always willing to help where needed. When she was "put out" she would make a little snorting sound, but she never used bad language. Both our parents were very careful in language usage. Mother was busy with hospital matron work and also at the Bible School, where her specialty was teaching the New Testament Epistles, but as I recall, she always had time for her kids. She introduced us early to good reading material and saw to it that there was plenty of it in the house. It was she, especially, who saw to our Christian training from the beginning. Later in life, as her physical strength waned, she became a "prayer warrior" for her children and grandchildren.

CHAPTER 10
MY HOME TOWN

*L*egaspi, though nowhere as large then as it is today (121,000+ in February 2000), was an up-and-coming city. It was the major, Pacific, deep-water port on Luzon and had a good pier and breakwater. Thousands of tons of copra (coconut meat for making oil) were shipped each year from Legaspi to countries all over the world. Before the war, loading the ships was usually done by cargadores—a "conveyor belt" of men, each with a large sack of copra on his shoulder.

Legaspi boasted a cinema (better pay someone to guard your car while you are in the theatre, or you chanced having your tires slashed, at the very least); a utilities plant (electricity was not always available); an ice plant; a central market place (Spanish style, where you could get all sorts of fruits, vegetables, meat, poultry and fish); lots of "Mom and Pop" stores carrying every kind of merchandise; and banks and various businesses headed by American or British nationals.

Up the road from Legaspi were located our mission hospital and the United Church (the pastor was a Filipino). There was also a mission residence located on the hospital grounds. This was called the "Mac house," since that's where the MacDonalds had lived before we came.

Prior to 1929, Uncle Mac (honorary uncle) oversaw the renovation of an existing Bible School dormitory to make the new hospital. He also had supervised the building of two more mission houses and a Christian Center with adjoining tennis courts and playgrounds on a compound about two kilometers up the road from the hospital. The "new" MacDonald house had a third floor, which had a large, screened, sleeping "porch." It was perhaps half as large in area as the floor beneath, and all their beds were there. Our homes in the Philippines all were open to the breezes, and we used mosquito nets at night. But, on this screened porch, nets were not necessary. We kids always enjoyed visiting overnight and enjoying the freedom of sleeping without nets. The MacDonalds and Smiths occupied the two reinforced concrete homes, while the LaPortes lived in an apartment on the second floor of the Christian Center, which they supervised. They later moved into the "Smith house" when the Smiths were reassigned to Manila.

The Christian Center was a large, two-story, reinforced concrete building which fronted on the main road just a short distance from the Normal School and the Provincial High School. Since most Filipino homes do not have the kind of living space we are used to in America, the mission provided a place for the students to come and study. A good library was available for their use, as well as for the general public. There were separate, smaller, study areas for those who needed a quiet place to do research or write papers. There was also a recreation area where the kids could play ping pong and such. It really was a center for the community. It was also definitely used as a mission outreach, with Christian literature and tracts at hand, and people, men and women volunteers, who were ready to talk to anyone who had questions.

MacDonalds and Smiths, and my mother, were involved in a training school for Christian lay men and women. Many towns and barrios had no resident pastor, and these lay evangelists and Bible women filled a definite need. The students came mostly from the provinces around us that made up the Bicol Peninsula, and from the Visayan Islands. One of the church activities where training was given was in Vacation Bible School (VBS) development. Every year a teachers' training institute would be held, where the teachers and helpers actually developed their lessons and crafts and taught them to each other. They even practiced the games to be played by the children. When I was eleven, I got to start being a helper at VBS, and I participated in the VBSs of 1940 and 1941.

CHAPTER 11
KID STUFF

We lived in the old "Mac house" from my birth until sometime in 1937 when I was eight years old. I remember just bits and pieces of those years. We had an amah to look after us until we were old enough to start school. As I recall, she was fairly permissive and allowed Dave and me all sorts of play—most of it imaginative, as I remember very few boughten toys. One of our favorites was playing tienda, where we would mimic the actions of the sellers and buyers. We would make cones of paper, fill them with proper amounts of sand, and "sell" them to each other. I remember once when Dave held the cone over his head (face up) to judge if I had "sold" him the correct amount. As often happens when you throw back your head, your mouth pops open. Well, his did, and just at that moment the cone disintegrated from the wet sand, and he really got a mouthful! Such sputtering! Mostly on the part of the amah!

While we little kids played our simple games, our older brothers, Bill and Allen, were constructing exciting things like a long rope rigged with pulleys from a high tree limb to a stump near the house. Attached to the rope-and-pulley contraption was a sort of hanging basket which they could pull up to the tree limb, climb in, and then let go for a thrilling ride down. I think Mother drew the line when they wanted to use Dave and me as passengers! All of the mission kids got together from time to time to play "capture the flag" and "kick the can," but mostly we played by ourselves or with Filipino friends when we were not in school. Sometimes, when we got to go up to the MacDonalds, the big boys would delight us smaller kids by bringing out large car tires to the lawn area. We little kids would curl up inside the tires and the big boys would roll us all over the lawn. We probably made quite a racket as we shrieked in anticipation of falling out.

The old "Mac house" was near the hospital. It was two storied with the upper level being living quarters for the mission family. There were wide, open-to-the-air, roofed porches along both the front and the back of the house. I suppose you might call them verandas. Stairways, front and back, led to the porches. The sala, a living/dining area, extended from the front porch to the back porch. On one side of the sala were three bedrooms, all connected. Tucked into an "L" in the sala was the fourth bedroom. Mom and Dad had the back bedroom; Ruth's and mine came in the middle; Allen and Dave shared the front bedroom, and Bill had the fourth bedroom until he sailed back to the U.S. in 1936. I can't remember how many bathrooms there were, but we had running water (most of the time) and electricity (most of the time). The toilets were the kind that had the water reservoir high up on the wall and you pulled a chain to let the water run into the bowl. The tap water was tepid at all times and didn't need to be heated for our showers. The cook had to heat water on the stove for washing dishes. The kitchen was upstairs in a separate, but attached, room just off the back porch. Our stove was kerosene and so was the refrigerator. For a time, I believe we had an icebox rather than a refrigerator. None of the houses I lived in had hot-water heaters.

Downstairs, behind the kitchen area and near the swimming pool, the folks had had a small nipa hut built for our playhouse. It was a typical country hut made of bamboo and nipa palm thatch and sat up on low stilts. A real bamboo ladder led to the front entry (no door), and there were several real window openings with let-down shutters. There I played for endless hours, and there, on my fifth birthday, in that same nipa hut, I embarrassed my mother in front of all the American kids and their moms who had been invited to the party. Mother had invited Betty James to bring down Patsy, and her little brother Peter, from Iriga for the celebration. The MacDonalds were there too. All was going just fine until we got to the gift opening part of the party! It was exciting—all those gifts for me! Then Peter James, just three years old, decided that since the package I held in my hand was the one HE had brought to give me, then HE should be the one to open the package. As I recall, we had quite a tussle, and not a little squalling! "Not for nothing" did I have the reputation

40

among the missionary kids (and grownups?) of being a cry-baby. Took me years to live it down!

Also, downstairs were the garage, storage area, laundry room, and living quarters for visiting dignitaries and/or servants, though our cook and houseboy, as well as the lavanderas (laundresses) lived in their own nipa homes. Quite a number of middle-class Filipinos (who also had house servants) lived in large homes, usually constructed of wood with corrugated tin roofs. Our home also had a corrugated tin roof, which yielded a pleasant patter of rain, with occasional leaks during a heavy monsoon rain. With that kind of rain, besides the patter of rain on the roof, you could hear the plinks and plunks of drops falling into various pails positioned strategically. Sometimes, in a particularly bad typhoon, the sheets of tin roofing would lift and fly off. These could be very dangerous if you were not in a protected area.

CHAPTER 12
STORMY WEATHER

The system of storm warnings in those days was quite rudimentary. For the residents of the area, who until the later 1930s did not even have radios, the only way to find out the threatened intensity of an approaching storm was to go down to the port of Legaspi and check out how many five-gallon cans had been hoisted on a rope at the weather station. The scale was much like our present-day categories, on a scale of one to five. Usually, our province escaped the worst storms and only suffered through a three-can or four-can typhoon. But, every few years we suffered through much more intense storms. We thought those storms were bad, but in those days we had no inkling of the cataclysmic storm of war which would sweep over all of Southeast Asia not many years hence.

When I was about five, I remember sitting out one four- or five-can typhoon, huddled in the dining area, which was the most protected area in our quarters. Our storm shutters were closed and latched but rattled constantly in the furious wind and rain. It was night, and we had a couple of candles burning at the dining room table. Electricity was out, of course. There were lots of leaks in the roof, but no panels had blown off. Suddenly, there was complete silence. We were in the "eye" of the typhoon. It was an eerie feeling. Then the storm started again, just as abruptly as it had stopped. After that storm we found much damage to our yard. Lots of branches had been snapped off. One coconut tree had its top blown off. That was the year when I found out about hearts of palm. When the top of a palm tree is blown off, it will die, so the best thing to do is cut it down and harvest the "heart" of the palm, which is just below where the palm fronds sprout. I think that one was a couple of feet long, and it was delicious!

Typhoons in the three-can and more category are very disastrous to the native economy. Many coconuts are blown off the trees. Fruit trees, such as papaya and banana, are either stripped of their fruit or destroyed completely. Many of the less sturdy homes are damaged or destroyed. Floods are an added burden. Although bananas bear only one stalk of fruit per plant, they send up many small plants around their base, and these reach bearing age in about a year. Papayas take only a little longer to bear fruit. But, it also may happen that an entire year's rice crop is decimated by flooding. Fishing may be affected, if for a lesser time. Since rice, fish, vegetables, and fruits are the main foods, a severe typhoon can bring much suffering. Bamboo and nipa thatch huts can be rebuilt fairly rapidly. Since the climate is warm, there is no problem with cold exposure, but such times are always difficult.

The large cement swimming pool behind our house was really a long, rect-angular, open, water-storage tank, although it was sometimes (rarely) used for swimming. But, it was mostly for use as our alternate water supply. With buckets of water we still had flush toilets! Drinking water, of course, had to be boiled after a severe storm, which would often disrupt the water supply. Otherwise, we had good water from the taps.

CHAPTER 13

EARLY GRADE SCHOOL DAYS

I have some vivid memories of my years in grade school. My first three grades were with the other mission kids where we were taught by our moms who used the Calvert system, a correspondence school curriculum utilized by diplomats and other Americans in foreign lands, and still advertised in National Geographic to this day. Somewhere in my first year or two of school I learned to read and took off from there! To this day I devour books, all kinds! We sort of envied the "big kids" who got to go to public school just down the road from the Christian Center compound where our little private school was held. But, my first year in public school was in Portland, Oregon.

In 1938 we took our one-year furlough in the States. There were six to seven years between furloughs, extended from the normal five years because of the Depression. Furloughs were exciting. Any number of months, perhaps even a year, before our scheduled sailing, the steamship company would send us a large picture of the liner, with all the cabins laid out on the various decks and carefully designated by first, second, and tourist classes. We always traveled by the least expensive mode, but we did get to choose our cabins (within parental limits). Ruth and I shared a cabin. I think Allen and David were in another, and Mother and Dad had the third. The trip would take about a month, with stops in Hong Kong, perhaps in Shanghai and some port in Japan, and in Hawaii on our way to the States. The staff was very attentive, and the kids on board had several stewards who were assigned specifically to them. We also ate meals at a different time from the adults, and we could order anything we wanted from the menu. I remember that I had frog legs once—not bad, but nothing to rave about either.

Our ship docked in San Francisco. I remember sailing UNDER the Golden Gate bridge, which had been opened only the year before. But, poor Allen had to view it from the porthole by his bunk. He had sprained his ankle badly the night before our arrival. He was taking the stairs two at a time when the ship, in the decided choppy current that flows north about twelve hours off shore, took an unexpected twist and down went Allen. He was confined to quarters for the balance of the trip. The rest of us all went up on deck to get a good look at this marvelous bit of engineering. We then took the train from San Francisco to Portland, where Mother's folks were living, so we could be near parents and grandparents for the year.

So, it was in Portland that I started fourth grade in a public school. We younger kids walked the five blocks to our school. I guess I'm fairly outgoing, since I didn't fear going to a new school in a totally different culture but rather looked forward to the experience. On that first day, I settled comfortably into my seat and looked around. My classmates, most of whom had been together since they were in first grade, gave me a good once over too. Meanwhile, the homeroom teacher was explaining what she wanted us to do when we wrote our papers or homework. She said we were to write our first names and then our last names in the upper-right-hand corner of our paper. I came to full attention! I have always been called Jean, but I knew that it was my middle name, not my first name. I knew my first name was Margaret, but I'd never been called that, much less seen it written anywhere! Oh, panic! Oh, embarrassment! Was I going to have to admit that I didn't know how to spell my name? Fortunately for me, the teacher chose to write my name on the board as an example. Thanks to phonics, I could READ my name, even though I had never seen it before. So, I was home free, and so relieved! I copied my name from the board, and never told a soul!

Our year in Portland held so many new and exciting things. Grandma taught me to darn socks. I saw my first snowfall and thought it was ashes coming from Mt. Hood. (After all, my only experience with drifting flakes was ash from Mt. Mayon in Albay Province.) I got to watch my two older brothers date a series of girls. They spent countless hours on the phone (if Mother didn't catch them at it). The only phone in the house was situated on the landing of

45

the staircase leading upstairs from the living room—not a very private place! And, of course, I just had to go up and down several times during a phone session! I'm told I was a regular pest. Brother Allen insisted in later years that I used to hide behind the couch in the evening and then pop up suddenly to blurt out, "That isn't the same girl you had here last night!" I don't remember that!

I do remember my first pair of roller skates, the tighten-with-a-key kind, and having sidewalks to skate on. No sidewalks in the provinces! There was a roller-skating rink with music and pretty lights a couple of miles from our house. Dave and I learned how to use the streetcars to get to the rink and also used the streetcars to go downtown to buy goldfish at Meier & Franks, the large department store. We'd bring them home in small, waxed, cardboard containers, sort of like the ones you get these days to take home food when you eat out at a Chinese restaurant. Mother allowed Dave and me to go on our various trips together without her supervision. Things were different in 1938–39. We never had any problems and cheerfully assumed that everybody went almost anywhere without any trouble. I was ten and David was eight years old that furlough year.

During furlough Dad took several courses to update his medical knowledge. He took the streetcar to his classes. The streetcar line was about two blocks from our house, and there was a slight hill to climb to get to it. Sometimes Dad would get a late start, and he would race up the hill, waving his arm and shouting "Para" or "sssss..st!" as the streetcar rolled by our corner. We kids got the biggest bang out of that!

Dad and Mother also were away on a "deputation" trip for several weeks, speaking at the various supporting churches in the Midwest. While they were gone, we were in the care of a family friend named Frankie. I wasn't too fond of her, since she insisted on serving cauliflower, which at that time I hated! All my life I've lived in a "clean plate" home. You eat what you take or are served—all of it!

Of course, in those Depression years, most everyone was glad to eat whatever was available. And, Portland had a marvelous Farmers' Market at the time. Dad used to take us kids there. He relished having all the buttermilk you could drink for five cents. We kids passed on that! Many fruits and vegetables, unknown and unavailable in the Philippines, were for sale. And, if you went late in the day, the prices were sharply reduced. That's the part my Scottish dad was especially good at—purchasing very ripe fruit for a low price. He would bring home several crates at a time! Mother was sometimes exasperated, as she hadn't planned on canning that evening. But, we ate well. Mom and Dad loved the peaches and cherries and pears. Dave and I longed for santols, baligan, mangos, and chicos! To each his own!

When I turned ten years old, I invited my entire class to my birthday party. One of the boys kept asking when the party was going to begin. What he meant was "when are the ice cream and cake going to be available?" Mother finally sent him to the grocery store a couple of blocks away to pick up the goodies she had previously ordered. Then the party "began!" Ruth's birthday is January 31, the day before mine. I don't remember her having a big party that year. In the Philippines, before the war, Mother often had the parties on the same day—with Ruth and her friends on the back porch and me and my friends on the front porch. How did Mother ever survive? It does help to have a cook and a houseboy!

In Portland, we got our first taste of doing our own housekeeping, though I'm sure Mother did most of it. I think we had to do dishes and make our own beds. Judging from a letter written by Grandpa in May of 1945, after he met us on our return from internment camp, he had been singularly unimpressed with my chances of turning out well from what he observed during our furlough year when I was nine! ("Care-free, work-detesting child," were his words!) However, by 1945 he noted a remarkable change, when he wrote his family, and said I was an "energetic, unselfish, reliable young girl, very sociable and helpful." What a difference seven years and a war can make!

Portland is a port city, though some 100 miles up the Columbia River from the Pacific coast. Large ships, particularly freighters, were often seen at the city docks, loading and unloading. As we passed over the Willamette River bridges on our way downtown, Mom and Dad observed with a great deal of distress the loading of ship after ship with scrap metal headed for Japan. The Chinese people in Portland often picketed these ships, since their country had been invaded by Japan in 1937 and had suffered much as the Japanese Army moved inland. Though we kids were largely unaware of all the implications, I do recall Mother's open questioning as to "if and when" we, in the Philippines, might be on the receiving end of some of this scrap metal.

CHAPTER 14

BACK HOME AGAIN!

---

*O*ur furlough-year ended in May 1939, and we returned home on a Canadian liner, the *Empress of Russia,* via Japan and China. The trip took about a month, and we encountered a heavy typhoon on the way, with huge waves that came up to the second deck. Dave and I were among the very few passengers using the dining room for several meals. It was fascinating to watch the silver and cutlery slide around the tables which had protective rims and dividers in place for rough weather. When we arrived home in Legaspi, we settled back into our familiar home in the "Richmond house."

I haven't really talked much about the Richmond house, though most of my pre-war memories are from those years 1937–1941 when we lived there. Dr. Richmond, an American physician who had come to the Philippines early in the 1900s had built the reinforced concrete home for himself and his wife several years before they retired back to the States. The mission board purchased his home for us, and the old "Mac" house (my early childhood home) was then utilized as housing for nurses and church workers. We moved into the Richmond house when I was seven or eight years old.

Two stories high, the Richmond house contained a complete apartment for visitors (living room, bedroom, and bath) downstairs in the front. Behind that apartment was the garage. A number of rooms—used as sleeping quarters, if needed, and for storage and laundry—were also located behind the front apartment. Outside, along the back wall, were two very large galvanized tin tanks to collect rainwater for use when necessary. They were connected to pipes which led directly from the roof gutters. These pipes entered through the top of the cans, and the water passed through screening to keep out bugs and mosquitoes. Faucets near the bottom let you collect the water in pails. Abundant tropical rain assured that those tanks never got empty, though they frequently overflowed.

The upstairs was reached by a broad inside staircase up from the front doors which opened off the covered entry. At the top, you immediately entered a long, wide expanse of space which was the sala. Doorways at the far end led to the galley which connected the kitchen and pantry to the rest of the house. Wide archways, to the left of the sala, opened onto the veranda, which was not screened. None of the large windows in the house were screened. In fact, they didn't have glass, either. They were open to whatever breezes might come along. Under the wide roof overhang, they were safe from rain, unless we had a typhoon. For typhoons we closed wooden shutters which let in some light through multiple small panes made of translucent

shell.

Richmond House, 1937–1941

Ruth's and my bedroom, with a walk-in closet, was at the front of the house and opened onto the porch. A connecting bath was between our bedroom and the study, which was David's bedroom before our furlough. Mother and Dad's bedroom came next to the study, on the other front corner of the house. There was a connecting bath between their bedroom and the third bedroom, which was Allen's. After our furlough, Allen stayed in the States, and David had Allen's old room. So, it was a square house, wrapped around the sala, with a kitchen attached to the galley porch at the rear. Steps led down from the galley porch, so we always had two exits.

Some vendors regularly came to the foot of the stairs at the back of our house, and Mother would go down and select the produce. As I recall, she always bought eggs and oranges from vendors. Eggs needed to be selected very carefully, as you might otherwise end up with a partially developed chick or two. The way Mother did that was to have a deep pan of water beside her. She would pick up the eggs, several at a time, and lower them into the water. If they lay on their sides they were fresh. If they stood on their ends, she refused to buy them. With the orange vendor, Mother often had to bargain, which is an accepted part of buying things in the Philippines. Some would call it haggling, but it was the system, and it worked.

All our ceilings were at least ten to twelve feet high to help create good ventilation. Since Legaspi is a lowland city, with lots of streams and also standing water in many places, we used mosquito nets to protect ourselves from malaria and dengue fever, both carried by mosquitoes. These nets were fastened at the top to a circular rod held up by an upright fastened to the head of the bed. Around the bottom of the net was a wide band of strong muslin cloth which could be tucked securely under the mattress after the bed's occupant, swishing a hand back and forth to shoo away any stray mosquito, climbed in. Mother was usually there to tuck us in, but we could do it ourselves if we had to. One of the houseboy's last jobs, before going off duty in the late afternoon, was to let down the nets over the turned down beds and tuck them in so they were tight before the mosquitoes started to come out from their daytime hiding places. If we were going to sit up on the porch awhile in the evening, we set coils of "punk" afire so that the smoke would discourage the mosquitoes.

Our houseboy, Angracio, had the job of polishing all our beautiful hardwood floors regularly. His method was to saw mature coconuts in half across the middle, trim the hard shell so that it wouldn't scratch the wood floor and smooth off the husks on the ends. Then, placing his feet securely on the half coconuts, he would skate all over the floors to buff them after he had cleaned and waxed them—ingenious and not easy to do, as we kids found out when we experimented with the skating process. The husks buffed the floors to a high shine, and they were cheap and bio-degradable to boot!

Angracio had many other duties around the house, but sometimes David and I could persuade him to take some time out to construct us a kite or two from bamboo and tissue paper. Those were wondrous affairs of all shapes and sizes. Filipinos do so many creative things with bamboo and tissue paper. For festivals there are always lanterns. Archways over the roads are constructed for just about any pleasant celebration or official visit. These are usually decorated with live flowers and leaves. Fiestas were always fun times, with decorations and marvelous specialty foods such as lechon (roast pig), pancit (a noodle dish with pork and shrimp), and suman (sweet sticky rice wrapped in banana leaves and steamed).

CHAPTER 15

GRADE SCHOOL—UPPER GRADES

Soon after our arrival home from our U.S. furlough, it was time to start school. Philippine schools run ten months a year. This year (1939) I entered public school, the only white person in my class of at least thirty kids. I was in fifth grade; David was in third grade; John and George MacDonald were also in that school. As far as I can remember, we were the only white kids in the entire student body.

This elementary school was associated with the Normal School (teacher training), but I don't remember having any student teachers when I was there. The principal was an American (his wife, also an educator, was the principal of the Provincial High School). All my teachers in both grades five and six were Filipinas (the -a ending indicates female; -o ending indicates male; a remnant of Spanish influence in the Islands).

Once a week—or was it every day? I don't remember—all the students lined up by class in front of the school building, and participated in the flag-raising ceremony. First was the American flag and then the Philippine flag. After that we would sing the national anthems from memory! Miss Navarez, the music teacher, would lead the singing. She would give us the pitch with her pitch pipe and start us off. At the end of the American national anthem, she would lower the pitch three steps and start the Philippine national anthem. I still remember almost all the words of the Philippine anthem (in English). Nowadays the Filipinos sing it only in Tagalog (pronounced "tah-GAH-loag"). School children sing it every morning when school is in session.

Land of the Morning, Child of the sun returning,
With fervor burning, Thee do our souls adore!
Land dear and holy, Cradle of noble heroes,
Ne'er shall invader Trample thy sacred shore!
Ever within thy clouds and through thy skies,
And o'er thy hills and sea,
Do we behold thy radiance, Feel the throb
Of glorious liberty.

Thy banner, dear to all our hearts,
Its sun and stars alight,
Oh, never may its shining field
Be dimmed by tyrant's might!

Beautiful land of love, Oh, land of light,
In thine embrace 'tis rapture to lie!
But it is glory ever, When thou art wronged,
For us, thy sons, To suffer and die!

We had the regular curriculum found in elementary schools in the States, with the addition of sewing, embroidery, and cooking in the upper grades. Reading, writing (legibility was very highly emphasized), and arithmetic were taught rigorously. Geography (world and Philippine) and history (Philippine particularly) rounded out our course of study. Testing was every six weeks, with report cards given out then. Reading speed and comprehension tests were frequent. Here I could really shine, since I loved to read anyway. Since English was my native language, I had much less trouble with comprehension than did my classmates.

We spoke only English at home. During my childhood, much to my later regret, I learned only a few polite Bicol phrases from my folks' friends and perhaps more than a few rude phrases from my friends. They all wanted to learn to speak better English and would not speak in the local dialect with me. Occasionally, on my way home from school, a group of boys would follow after me yelling, "White rabbit!" I have to admit that contrary to turning the other cheek, I usually hollered back, "Brown dog!" I wonder how much damage I did to Christ's cause through my actions? Today I would probably be hauled into court!

Our physical education in public grade school consisted of group exercise periods at times during the week. I suppose we did jumping jacks and such, but I don't have a clear recollection. I do, however, remember my mortification when I was singled out of our girls' group and made to stand in front of everybody while the teacher tugged and pulled at my black bloomers, which Mother had had made to the teacher's specification. Everybody in class was supposed to wear bloomers during exercise period, but Mother's prompt compliance with the edict meant that I was the first in the class to do so. Therefore, I was put on display (or rather the bloomers I was wearing were put on display) so that the rest of the girls could urge their mothers to get with the program!

Fifth and sixth grade girls had home economics classes. Along with embroidery, we learned crocheting and tatting—all skills used by many women in their homes to make those beautiful, delicate, baby clothes and blouses so desired by American women. It was a way for them to make a living. I enjoyed embroidery, but somehow I often mislaid my crochet hook, and so I didn't do too well on that. Embroidery was a lot more interesting to me.

Cooking lessons came in sixth grade. It seemed a great shame to me that our text was one with American recipes, since most Filipinos do not eat that kind of food, even if they can afford it. But, nevertheless, we read about roasts and gravy, mashed potatoes and casseroles, cookies and mincemeat pies. We didn't make all of those things, thank goodness. Once in a while though, we did do a bit of cooking from carefully selected recipes. I remember one day, when our class had a substitute teacher who hurried into the room at the last minute. Our recipe for the day was griddle cakes. The teacher flipped the book open to the right page and said, "Today we are going to make GIRDLE [sic] cakes." (Yes, she pronounced it that way several times!) I clamped my mouth tightly shut and kept listening. Far be it from me to correct a teacher! So, each team got out the bowls and the beaters and the ingredients as the teacher read each direction from the lesson. We industriously sifted and creamed and beat . . . and waited for the next direction. But, the teacher was feeling pretty confident by now, and she continued, without checking the recipe, "Well, it's cake, so I guess we need to get out the cake pans. I don't see any oven temperature, but about 350 degrees should be correct." The girls looked a little mystified, but we all did what we were told to do. I kept my own counsel. Soon there were three cake pans, each half full of batter, shoved into the hot oven. We cleaned up our messes and stood around to see what was next.

Now the teacher did look at the textbook and became a little worried, for there, plain to see, were the directions: "When brown on one side, turn over." She peeked into the oven, and turned slightly pale. There were the three pans of partially baked batter which had risen in the pan, but not evenly! Each pan had three or four "volcanoes" thrust up from the batter. How were we to "turn them" over? She decided to let them bake a little longer to firm them up and then we gently removed the pans from the oven to see what we could do. Well, we tried, with our pancake turners, to "flip" the cakes, which, of course, came to pieces. Most of the dough did fall back into the cake pans, and the results were put back in the oven to finish baking. The teacher was shaking her head, and we girls were not too happy either since it was taken for granted that whatever we cooked we ate! Even with syrup they were awful! Probably my classmates still wonder what is so good about American griddle cakes!

Some time during my sixth-grade year, my eyesight became very bad. No one had noticed anything unusual, but one day when the teacher was writing the assignment on the board, I could see her hand moving but could not make out even one letter. Being the tallest girl in the class, I always had to sit in the back. I thought maybe if I were nearer to the board, I would be able to copy down the assignment. The teacher allowed me to move to a front seat, but things were not much better, and the letters were blurry at best.

My folks, on being informed of the problem, arranged for me to have an eye exam at Schofield Army Hospital in Manila. Mother took me up on the train, and we spent several days there having various tests and getting the prescription filled. Near-sightedness and astigmatism! What a blow! Now I had to wear glasses all the time. It was nice to be able to see well though! That was one trip to Manila I sort of enjoyed. All that attention and I got to have ice cream sodas in a store on the Escolta in downtown Manila! Sodas are heavenly! It was on that trip that Mother and I discovered that somehow I had also developed a taste for coffee.

CHAPTER 16

BUT, THERE'S MORE TO LIFE THAN JUST SCHOOL!

I've always been interested in most any food and its preparation. At the Richmond house there was an outside cook shed (not in any way associated with our house kitchen). There Dave and I spent many happy hours learning to cook Filipino-style rice in clay pots, with banana leaves to line the pot, and gulay (pronounced "GOO-lie) which could consist of a variety of meats or fish along with vegetables and often finished off with coconut milk we made from scratch.

The way you make coconut milk is simple, if you have the right equipment. First, get a ripe (mature) coconut (the water inside will swish when you shake the nut). This nut will have had the husk removed already. Hold the nut in your left hand so that the "eyes" face toward your wrist.

Do this over a sink or outside over the ground. Crack the nut open along the center (equator) of the nut, using the dull side of your bolo (long machete type of knife, made from old car springs) and let the clear water run out. If you don't have a bolo, you can use a hammer, but the nut will not crack as cleanly. Grate the firm, white, coconut meat. Graters are made from lengths of wrought iron on which one end is flattened into a round flat head into which teeth are filed. The tail end of the grater is fastened to a sawhorse or something to hold it up from the ground. You sit "sidesaddle" on the saw-horse, place the half coconut over the grater head, and commence to shred the meat into a pan which you have placed below. It takes a while, and a few scratches on your wrists, to get the knack of grating coconut.

When you have grated all the meat from the shell, you are ready to make the coconut milk. We usually did two squeezings. For the first time through, pour several cups of water over the grated meat in the pan. With your hands (clean, of course) squeeze the meat and water to express the "milk." Then take up double handfuls of the meat and squeeze as hard as you can to get all the moisture out. Put this meat in another pan. Repeat squeezing the remaining meat until most of the shredded coconut is removed from the milk. Strain that milk through several layers of cheesecloth into a container. That's the best milk. Then pour two cups or less of water over the squeezed meat and repeat the whole process. The second squeezing is still good, but not as rich as the first squeezing. Coconut oil is usually made from the first squeezing only. But, that's a whole other lesson!

David and I did all our "native" cooking over open fires in the cook house. Rice, fish and gulay were our favorites. Gulay is cooked in a kawali (an iron wok) which has a rounded bottom and fits well on three stones. That's what our "burners" were—three large stones (DON'T take them from a riverbed! The water-soaked rocks might explode!) to hold the cooking utensils. There is an art to knowing just when to pull back enough sticks and coals so that the rice does not burn but will still continue to cook to doneness. In all our play we never gave a thought to the idea that someday we might be called on to cook rice and gulay for a bunch of American refugees.

We also experimented with our favorite dessert of bebingka, a sweet made from rice and wheat flour, baking powder, sugar, and coconut milk, stirred into a thick batter and poured into an empty oval sardine can (the large one) lined with banana leaf. Now came the tricky part. We would cover the can with another banana leaf, carefully balance the pan on three stones over fairly hot coals and then place a flat piece of tin (the top of a five-gallon can was just right) over the top of the sardine can and contents. Then add some coals to the top of the sheet of tin, and voila, an oven of sorts, with heat on top and bottom! Such wonderful fragrance came from our efforts, though I'm sure we had many a flop before we mastered some of the common items.

As I recall, no one stood over us to "train" us to cook Filipino style. We learned by visiting our cook's family in his home quite near our house. Dave and I would often be there to watch the food preparation, though Mother felt it was "imposing" for us to stay for meals. Their "stove," unlike the one in our cook shed, was actually a sand box about eight to twelve inches deep and raised on legs so that when the stones were placed the pots would be at a convenient level for cooking. Depending on the size of the sand box, you could have two or three or more "burners." Dave's and my stove had two, and we used them often. Fuel was wood or charcoal. Mother and Dad seemed to have counted on our using good sense with our fires, and we seemed to have deserved that trust.

CHAPTER 17
FUN TIMES

*I*n those days before the war we usually made up our own games. Until I was twelve, I climbed trees with almost as much ease as younger brother David. Sometimes when we got home from school we would climb the tall santol tree, gather the peach-shaped fruit, and rush out to our front gate to sell the fruit to the high school kids walking home from their classes, which let out later than ours. We didn't need the money, but it was our version of front-yard lemonade stands. On a Saturday we might be out at the road bright and early to buy fish from the vendors going by with the night's catch. Our favorite fish was cibobog, and they came in various lengths from three inches to seven or eight inches. When our cook prepared the little ones for our suppers, he would split and "butterfly" them, dip them in cornmeal, and fry them crisp. Served with calamansi (tiny round lemons) and steamed rice, nothing could be better! Our whole family was partial to them.

Sundays were quiet at our house. We attended Sunday School at the Bicol church. It had English classes as well as those in dialect. Some years I got to be in Mother's class. Once in awhile, we kids were obliged to stay for the Bicol service. We could sing along, although we didn't understand the words we were reading. During the sermon I usually read through favorite books of the Bible. I got well acquainted with Ruth, Esther, and the Judges during Bicol services. Since I was quiet and sat with my head bowed (reading), probably everybody thought I was a good little girl! I hoped so. During my twelfth year, I joined the church.

If we were excused from church service after Sunday School, we rushed home (walking, of course) to get in on the traditional Sunday ice cream making. Feling would have made up the thin custard and then "built" a particular ice cream from that base. My favorite was "lumbud" (very young coconut) ice cream. The flesh is almost jelly-like in texture and can be easily spooned out of the shell. It is fairly sweet and very tasty. In ice cream, it's heavenly. Sometimes Feling would mash ripe avocados and add them to the basic mixture. Although I didn't care for avocados plain (we had five bearing avocado trees in our yard), I was rather partial to avocado ice cream. Usually, though, we had plain vanilla or chocolate ice cream. Angracio would be well on the way to finishing up cranking the ice cream by the time we got home from Sunday School, and we kids could get in on the exciting part of licking the dasher! Then more ice would be packed around the top and the whole freezer covered with gunnysacks before being set aside for the ice cream to harden. We had a large freezer, a five-quart-size if I recall correctly, and we usually managed to do away with all of the ice cream during the course of the dinner and afternoon.

Feling and Angracio had a half-day off on Sundays, so our big meal was always at noon. Often we had roast chicken, which Dad proceeded to dissect with deliberation and anatomical discussion. Almost any roast that included bones was treated the same way, and sometimes we got a little impatient waiting for our plates to be served. I suppose we had potatoes too, though I much preferred rice (and still do). Mother made up the menus and went over the week's work with Feling, who would then purchase the necessary foods from day to day. We did have a refrigerator, but it was not huge. It, and our cook stove, both run by kerosene, had legs that sat in shallow pans filled with kerosene to keep out the ants. You had to be careful to keep anything, such as a broom or mop, from leaning up against the refrigerator or stove since the ants invariably would find their way to their goal!

Sunday afternoons we were allowed no active games of any sort—no competitions or spending time with playmates. Mostly we read books. Our home was well supplied with books of all kinds and for all ages. I read through the Oz books and Tarzan books several times. We had a full set of My Bookhouse which contained the classics. We also had story books about missionaries and other heroes of faith. Dad and Mother usually took a long siesta in the heat of the day. Feling, after cleaning up from Sunday dinner, left for his afternoon off.

Then Ruth and I could invade his kitchen! We could bake anything we wished, the only proviso being that we left the kitchen exactly as we found it. No exceptions!

If I didn't want to read or bake something, I often wandered out in the back yard to look at all the interesting bugs and things. There was a certain kind of fat, smooth caterpillar, bright green with red tips on horn-like projections from his body, which was as big around as my thumb and about three to four inches long. These critters loved the avocado leaves, and since we had five trees, I could often find them munching away. In time, they would spin their cocoons, and that's when it got exciting! I would get several cocoons, hanging from their twigs, and carefully place them in a large glass container covered with cheesecloth and then watch and wait. Sure enough, eventually out came the most beautiful large moths—so pretty and velvety! I always let them go when their wings dried.

Mother said that I always liked insects of all varieties and even when I was only two would often squat down and say, "Oh, look at the pretty bug!" We had lots of bugs in the Philippines, many of them with iridescent coloring. The butterflies were numerous and varied. Some of the kids had butterfly collections. And, of course, there were the ubiquitous house lizards. They were usually from three to five inches long, light brown in color, and great at catching insects. Only once in awhile would they lose their grip on the ceiling and plop down beside you or on you. Outside we had the bigger, green geckos. Mostly they stayed in the trees and you could hear them call to each other during the night.

Then there were the other bugs, such as centipedes, cockroaches, leeches, ants and termites! Mostly we left them alone, and they (except for cockroaches and leeches) left us alone. Termites were probably the most destructive, though cockroaches were a close second. Our kind of termites in the Philippines didn't like light, so they would build themselves tunnels of masticated wood (sort of a sawdust-like material) to get where they wanted to go. They were pretty sneaky! Sometimes, before you were aware that there were any around, you would suddenly find a low brown tunnel leading to a trunk or a bookcase or anywhere there was something the termites enjoy eating! Any trunks filled with clothing or stored papers, if left on the floor and not regularly moved and inspected, were fair game!

Cockroaches were partial to food crumbs or any pasty-type substance. I had been given a life-size baby doll when I was one or two. I named it "Peaz Pack" for some unknown reason, and carried it everywhere. Peaz Pack had a stuffed cloth body and limbs, but his head was made from the pasty substance, molded, and then painted to show face and hair. He was just the right size to wrap up and use for the Baby Jesus in the Christmas pageants each year. But, the cockroaches loved his head, and over the course of a few years, they ate off the whole top of his head! I cried.

Cockroaches were everywhere in the Philippines! They were big ones, often two inches or more. And, they could fly! I believe that since our main export crop was copra we had an extra supply of cockroaches, since they seemed partial to copra and the coconut debris associated with that. We were not plagued with them at home so much since everything they liked was in airtight cans or jars. But, I remember one trip Mother took with Ruth and me. It was on an inter-island freighter, headed for the smaller island of Catanduanes, north and east of our province. Mother had some church business there and took us along as companions. The ship was loaded with all sorts of produce and animals in baskets and sacks and woven containers, or even tethered. There were lots of passengers too, and the ship was very crowded, not at all unusual for a Filipino ship. The captain thought he was doing us a favor when he offered the use of his own cabin to the three of us. But, we found two things when we tried to settle down for the overnight trip. One was that with the door closed it was stifling hot in the cabin. The other was that with the door closed the cockroaches had nowhere to go but 'round and 'round the cabin! We did not enjoy our night!

Anywhere you went you could see inch-wide trails of ants headed only they knew where, but busy, busy, busy! Right by my sand pile (black sand was all I had seen until I was about ten years old) were several ant trails. Across the drive was the low hedge which bore small lavender trumpet-shaped flowers. Each flower had a drop of nectar at the base of the trumpet, and if you pulled it off the bush very carefully, you could sip the nectar before it ran out. I remember that I used to demarcate a "cemetery" of a square meter or so in my sand pile and then sit there and reach out to the ant trail, squash an ant, bury it, carefully pick one of those small lavender flowers, sip the bit of nectar, and then place it on the "grave" until my "cemetery" was filled. Now that may be gross, but it was imaginative!

Another favorite use of my sand pile was more directly connected to my observation of my surroundings. Mt. Mayon loomed large in our lives, producing steam, smoke, and hot rocks which sometimes were tossed above the rim of the crater. We could often see a glowing tip at night. About every ten years or so the volcano would manage a very impressive eruption. We had numerous earthquakes associated with all this activity. Taking the mountain, for my example, I would construct a "volcano" of wet sand, placing a large stick horizontally at the base extending into the middle and a smaller stick standing vertically from the tip of the other stick. Then, I would pack the sand as tightly as possible and form my perfect cone of Mt. Mayon. Then, carefully, carefully, I would remove the vertical stick and then the horizontal stick, hoping that the openings would remain intact. Before the whole thing could collapse, I would bring a burning stick from the cook shed and gently insert it through the horizontal opening. Sure enough, from the top of the "mountain" would come forth a wonderful plume of smoke. This was neat, and very safe, except for the time or two when I forgot to remove the hot stick, and walked barefoot over my collapsed mountain.

CHAPTER 18
MORE MEMORIES

*F*or Sunday supper we usually had cold salads, which Feling had prepared earlier. Then we headed off for English church, which was held every Sunday evening in the large auditorium upstairs at the Christian Center. Dr. LaPorte was the minister of that church. Many Filipinos, especially the professionals and the Bible School students, who were quite proficient in English, attended, along with all the missionaries and their kids and any other American or British citizen who happened to be in the area. The "pews" were benches, made of slats with wide openings between the pieces, so that my legs were "striped" before the service was over. No wonder I wiggled! The sermons tended to be long and the prayers even more interminable. But, the singing was great, and Auntie Margaret (MacDonald) was a wonderful pianist. As I grew older, I got more out of the services. I do remember that Dr. LaPorte frequently preached on the "last times." Preachers today still do.

Auntie Margaret taught all of us kids piano. I took lessons from age six to twelve and am sorry now that I did not apply myself with more diligence! She would hold recitals for her students in the same auditorium where English church was held. I hated recitals! My sister Ruth did much better than I at music lessons and even played the organ later when she was in her teens.

I wasn't too adept at any music that had lots of runs and trills, but I really liked the plain, four-part-hymn melodies, and practiced them with gusto. When I was eight or so, I remember learning the hymn *Wonderful Words of Life.* It had lots of repetition and many octave chords. I could really bang it

64

out and tried to memorize it so that I could play it with my eyes closed. For some reason, as a child, I often thought that someday I might be blind and that I needed to have some music memorized—a childish fancy but it provided motivation. Today, at age 72, I can still play that hymn with my eyes closed.

That Christian Center auditorium was put to multiple use. Often, on a Friday night, there would be a sort of Talent Night for the congregation. How the Filipinos loved to spoof their beloved missionaries. They could make up some really good ones about Dad. One of the most memorable was done by shadow plays, using several large white sheets as a screen with a very bright exam light behind them. As the audience watched, a gurney was rolled onto the stage. The patient was viewed as an exaggerated lump on the gurney, with a sheet draped over him. In strolled the surgeon. Then nurses appeared, rolling in the instrument trays. All of this, of course, in silhouette, as we watched with bated breath to see what would happen next.

Each time, something outrageously funny would be portrayed by the actors—all silent, naturally, and done in very slow motion to get the most out of the action. Sometimes the doctor would pull meters and meters of gut out of the abdomen. Or, perhaps an instrument would not be what the surgeon wanted and the poor nurses would wilt under the wrath and scorn. Sometimes the patient would start to come out of anesthesia before the operation was over, and that would add to the confusion as the attendants tried to keep him on the operating table. Occasionally, the patient would almost expire. Then came such a flurry of listening for a heartbeat and injecting of medications. These pantomimes usually brought down the house, Dad laughing just as hard as anyone else.

CHAPTER 19

HIGH SCHOOL

I became a high school freshman in 1941 at the age of twelve. The system which had been set up by the Americans for elementary schools in the Philippines had consisted of grades one through seven until early in 1941. That year the legislature and President Quezon passed and signed a bill decreasing the elementary grades to six. 1940–41 was the year I was in sixth grade, so my class graduated at the same time that the seventh graders did (much to their disgust!).

There were only 400 seats for incoming freshmen at our Provincial High School. It was the only public high school in the entire province. Anyone who wanted to go on to high school had to take a competitive written examination. That year, since there were double graduating classes from the elementary schools all over the province, there were more than 1000 of us who took the exam. I remember that I took it shortly before we left for our vacation time in Baguio, and I wondered if I would pass or if I would utterly disgrace my family and my country by missing out entirely on the chance to enter high school. All who took the tests were Filipinos except for John MacDonald and me. What a relief when I learned that I had placed 63rd. John came in first! I comforted myself with the thought that he had a whole year more of learning than I did! There were forty students in each of ten classes, placed according to standing in the general exam. John was in the first section, and I was in the second, so we never had classes together.

Physical Education in Philippine high schools does not offer the variety available here in the States. The boys could take track and field. I believe there might have been some team sport, such as soccer, but no intramural sports. Everything was outside, as we did not have a gym. The girls had only two choices: folk dancing or track. Folk dancing, very beautiful and pleasant to watch when performed by graceful Filipinos, has some very basic foot and hand movements. They are, for the most part, slow and languid movements, nothing like the hulas of Hawaii, much less the frantic movements of the Tahitian dances. All the girls in school had P.E. during the same late afternoon period. They would line up, military fashion, by class, put an arm's length between themselves, and then try to duplicate the movements of the various folk dances by following the leaders who stood at the front. One look at that and I opted for track, enjoying the hurdles the most. It was my track coach who sent me to the hospital one afternoon when I was having unusual pain in my lower abdomen while running or jumping hurdles.

CHAPTER 20

MILWAUKEE HOSPITAL

---

*I*n the years before "the war" (which is what my generations call WWII), our mission hospital had no such things as respirators or any other machine which would require a constant source of electricity. The hospital did have an emergency generator which was necessary for refrigeration of spoilable medicines and to provide lighting for such surgeries that might be required while the electricity was out. This happened more frequently than one would wish, especially during typhoons. Dad did not even have a fluoroscope to use in the mission hospital until 1939, when we returned from a one-year furlough in the States.

However, it was a modern hospital in every respect for that area of the world. The private rooms were upstairs at the front of the hospital, with storerooms and pharmacy across the hall and the operating room jutting out in a separate wing facing north for the best natural light to augment the electric lights. Separate wards for men and women, reception area, offices, and kitchen were on the ground floor.

Dad was well known for his surgical skill, and a number of graduates of the University of the Philippines Medical School came to Milwaukee Hospital for residency training. There was a well-qualified staff of registered nurses, assisted by trained aides. An evangelist and Bible woman completed the staff. Mother was "matron" and kept track of all sorts of things. In the years just before the war, hospital staff members used to go out to the barrios on a rotating schedule to hold health and wellness clinics and do evangelistic work.

The laboratory, also located on the first floor, was equipped with a dental chair, where I spent a number of uncomfortable hours. However, there were certain unique distractions to keep your mind off the drilling. The dentist used a pedal-operated drill powered by foot similar to the old sewing machines. Directly in view of any patient in the dental chair were Dad's lab specimens carefully preserved and labeled. My most distinct memory of that view was a series of glass bottles containing miscarried fetuses, from about one month through several months. The bottles got bigger and bigger as needed. Eventually, I too had a part of me briefly on display in that room!

In the late summer of 1941 when my track coach at high school told me that I needed to have Dad check me out, I headed cheerfully for my familiar haunts. Dad diagnosed chronic appendicitis, but when the pain worsened abruptly, he pushed up the surgery schedule, even though Mom, in Manila on business, wouldn't be home until that evening.

Dr. Reyes, a new resident, was Dad's assistant since Dr. Ago, the senior resident on staff, was out in the barrios with the mobile clinic. Several registered nurses formed the rest of the operating team. As was his custom, Dad prayed aloud, right there in the Operating Room with me and the staff before beginning the surgery. Since Dad had no one qualified to administer ether, he always opted for spinal anesthesia, and was very adept at administering it. Although this particular vial of anesthesia was not completely effective, it was enough to enable Dad to perform surgery with just a little more local stuff. Of course, I was wide awake and rather annoyed that Dad insisted on raising a screen between my face and the surgical area. I wanted to watch! (No, I didn't think too much about the danger of spreading my germs over the operative field. I just wanted to see what was going on!)

Dad always encouraged the residents to participate as fully as possible, and I remember feeling some dull poking and prodding as Dr. Reyes tried to identify and isolate the appendix! Dad got a little impatient, since appendectomies usually didn't take very long. However, it seems that my appendix was so swollen that it looked like a piece of small intestine instead of the little worm-like appendage! But, then it was located and Dad soon had it out and closed me up quickly. I felt great and wanted to walk to my room, but the nurses prevailed on me to submit to being wheeled on the gurney. In those years, the standard practice was to keep you in bed for about five days! The nurses didn't even want me to turn over in bed by myself, but Dad was more up-to-date and allowed as much activity as I wanted and could do. Meanwhile, my grossly enlarged appendix, six inches long and bigger around than a man's thumb, was carefully "pickled" and put on display in the laboratory.

Day one, two, and three passed uneventfully. Mother came back from Manila, and I was feeling perky and progressing in my diet. But, late on the third night, I started to have rather severe abdominal pain. The night nurse wanted to send a messenger to my dad, but I prevailed on her to wait until the morning, when he would be there at 7:00 a.m. During day four, the pain was unremitting. Evidently, that distended appendix had leaked some bad germs into the abdomen before my surgery. I was in serious trouble. Dad consulted with the other doctors on staff, read the literature on my symptoms, and I believe he also consulted with the doctors at the provincial hospital. Reluctantly, he had to come to the diagnosis of peritonitis, in those years usually fatal. However, the sulfa drugs had come out on the market a year or so before, and he did have a supply of tablets and powder. By then, I was sort of out of it (pain shots, I suppose, but my memories are hazy at best).

The following day (fifth post-op from the appendectomy) Dad opened me back up, assisted by Dr. Reyes as well as by Dr. Ago who had returned from clinic duty. Peritonitis is what they found in full swing! They cleaned me out and poured in the sulfa powder, put in drains (five or six in all, from various parts of me) and closed me up. (I can't imagine how my dad felt, having to operate on his own child!) The doctors prayed. The missionaries and their families prayed. Members of the local congregation prayed. Telegrams to mission headquarters alerted them to the problem, and all over the Philippines prayers went up for my recovery, if it be God's will. I am told that it was touch and go for several days. I don't remember. I was aware enough once to observe Dad giving me a blood transfusion, 50 cc at a time, while the nurse held the basin containing the blood and kept stirring it slowly so it wouldn't clot. Mom gave the blood. (Years later we learned that she and I have the same blood type and Rh factor.) Within the next day or two I had "turned the corner" and was on my way to recovery.

God is merciful! In a week or two, in early October of 1941, I went home, carefully holding the bottle with my "pickled" appendix. I wanted to show it to my two aunts (both nurses) in the States one day. Within a few weeks, I returned to school in time to take my triad (six-week exams). Since I had missed class most of those weeks, I think I didn't do too well, but I must have passed. My strength gradually returned, though I had to sit on the sidelines and watch my classmates train for a track meet.

CHAPTER 21

HOLIDAYS AND PARTIES

---

*W*e Americans almost always had a Halloween party and often made it a costume party. We'd play spooky games, and probably Uncle Smith would tell spooky stories, and then we would have to go through the haunted house! I remember having my hand plunged into slimy spaghetti (brains!) and bowls of peeled grapes (eyeballs). What yelps and smothered laughter! And, the costumes! All were homemade, of course, and most were in the season's theme. Some were downright funny.

I remember the party hosted by MacDonalds one year. All the Americans in town had been invited. Mr. and Mrs. Monto, a fairly staid couple, who headed up the Normal School and the High School were invited too. They had one son, Sandy. (I suppose his real name was Alexander.) None of us kids knew them well at all, though Sandy attended our small private school. A whole bunch of us, including the Montos, arrived for the party at about the same time. We had to park some distance from the front door since other guests had arrived earlier. It was pretty dark as we trooped up the driveway to the front door together. When we got under the porch light, I was startled and amazed to see sedate Mr. Monto, who was not too tall, and somewhat rotund, costumed as a "Baby"—diaper, romper pants, bonnet, and big bottle with a nipple! He took a lot of ribbing and seemed to have a great time acting silly. I never forgot the scene. But, even more funny was meeting him again in Springfield, Illinois, in 1947, where he was a professor in the lower division of the seminary my husband was attending. I almost swallowed my tongue when

I first recognized him. You can imagine the picture that came to my mind!

The totally American holiday of Thanksgiving was always a joint affair. The mission families took turns hosting the meal for any and all Americans in the area—business people, Army officers who were training a company of Philippine Scouts, the American educators, as well as all the missionaries in the Bicol Provinces.

I can recall quite a number of Thanksgiving Days, but perhaps the most clear in my memory is the one in November of 1941, which was held at our house. We had a long table set up in sort of an "L" shape, and I got to decorate down the center. The tropical climate does not allow for "fall colors" (having only one season), but we had plenty of croton bushes which bear variegated leaves all year long, so those would be my autumn leaves. No grapes grow in that hot, moist climate, so I would use yellow lanzones, which actually grow on trees but form bunches, somewhat looser than grapes but close enough to pretend. Those fruits and foliage, along with candles, would be the decorations for the Thanksgiving table. There were all the traditional Thanksgiving foods. (Yes, we had turkeys in the Philippines!) Feling had outdone himself and everyone was replete.

But, it was a rather somber group of adults who sat around the table with coffee or tea after dinner. The Army men were assuring the rest of them that IF an attack came, they would be back to take care of the situation. They had been ordered to move toward Manila, and Legaspi would have no defense at all if they couldn't make it back. Our mission staff had been augmented during the year with missionaries who had been withdrawn by the Presbyterian Board from their former stations in Manchuria, China, and Japan, and sent to the Philippines to be "safe" until any conflict might be over and they could return to their stations. The Japanese had controlled Korea for a number of years, and from there had moved north into Manchuria. They had invaded China in 1937, and many were the stories of terror and hardship there. In Japan itself, Americans were being treated with more and more hostility. Only the Philippines, with its large American and Filipino Army seemed to be a safe place. Dr. and Mrs. T. Cook were from Manchuria; Rev. D. Martin came from Japan; and Miss D. Hendricks had been in China. My Uncle Albert, Dad's brother, had been evacuated from Korea early in 1941. His wife and sons had returned to the States even before that. However, Albert was stationed in Manila "for the duration."

CHAPTER 22

GOD REST YE MERRY GENTLEMEN!

We always looked forward to Christmas with great excitement. Every year, months before the date, large mysterious packages would begin to arrive in the mail. Pan Am Clippers started trans-Pacific service in 1936, but package postage was prohibitive. Surface mail took a month or more to arrive in Manila from the States, and then it took several days or weeks more to get to the provinces. Our relatives in the States would send our presents early, maybe in July or August. Those usually arrived in September or early October. Dad and Mother ordered stuff from the Sears catalog, and those Christmas boxes would come too, usually along about the same time.

The packages would be hidden away in the hall closet, but as Christmas grew closer, the boxes would come out to be admired and prodded. Then, after a few days, the shipping box would be opened and the individual packages brought to light. Not until just before Christmas were the packages placed under the decorated Christmas tree (a long-needle pine that grew on the slopes of Mt. Mayon, and which was carefully selected by family members who hiked up to get the tree). Then we were free to pick up the packages, shake them, feel them, and speculate endlessly as to what was in them. Christmas morning we could empty our socks, hung on a mock fireplace made out of cardboard cartons and brick-patterned crepe paper, but we could not open our "real" presents until everybody was up. Dad distributed the gifts from under the tree. We kids used to think the folks dawdled on purpose on Christmas morning!

But, Christmas of 1941 was going to be far different for us all!

PART TWO

CHAPTER 23

WAR!

Land dear and holy, Cradle of noble heroes,
Ne'er shall invaders Trample thy sacred shore!
Thy banner dear to all our hearts, Its sun and stars alight,
Oh, never may its shining field Be dimmed by tyrant's might!

*P*earl Harbor Day for us was Monday, December 8, 1941, since the Philippines is on the other side of the International Date Line. That day we went to school as usual, though there was tension in the air. On Tuesday and Wednesday, many of the students whose parents' barrios were far removed from Legaspi were starting to head back home until the situation cleared. Everyone knew of the Japanese bombing of Clark Field, and our school administration decided that we needed to practice evacuating the building in case of a bombing attack in our area. Our assigned "safe" spot was a ravine just behind the school buildings, and by the time we had a couple of drills in a day, not much time or energy was spent on scholastics. Thursday, December 11, more than half the student body was absent.

Earlier in the week, Dad had purchased and stored (under our main stairway in the house!) about fifty five-gallon-cans of gasoline to take us through the crisis. Mother would not rest until he had Vicente and our houseboy construct a lockable shed at a considerable distance behind the house, down in a sort of ravine which ran behind our backyard, in which the volatile gas could be stored.

The missionaries had also drawn up tentative plans for evacuation in case of a bombing. Of course, all believed (or hoped) that it would be a temporary sojourn just until our armed forces returned and took care of the situation. As we headed to bed that night, everything seemed as normal as possible in tense times under a total blackout. My sister Ruth tells me that Mother had, on Pearl Harbor Day, packed a small suitcase with a change of clothes and a small wrapped Christmas gift for each of us "just in case," but I didn't know that then.

Then came the morning of December 12! After David and I worked up nerve enough to wake up the folks before 6:00 a.m., action was swift and bewildering to us kids. Mother told us to gather up whatever clothes and such as we could carry. Dad ran downstairs to wake Aunt Olive, who happened to be staying overnight with us, and told her to grab her stuff and get her car ready. She informed him that she was not budging until she had had her morning shower. So, in a huff, he ran back upstairs and helped to get us ready to leave. It seemed that we were not going to go together as a family. Rather, we three kids would go with Aunt Olive to Iriga (not the place chosen by the other missionaries) and Mother would follow later on the bus (though she thought she was going to stay with Dad). Dad, who had delivered a baby via caesarian section for one of the hospital nurses just the day before, felt he must stay with his hospital patients, few though they were.

I remember sitting in the back seat of Aunt Olive's car in our garage, clutching my small clothes bag, while Mother thrust in the small suitcase she had prepared and all the last minute supplies she could think of through the open car windows. I distinctly recall a five-pound box of cheese that came tumbling into my lap. Also, Mother made sure we had our Bibles along. Quick hugs, and then we were off. No time for tears! But, I remember that my chest felt as if it had a big lump of lead in it.

CHAPTER 24

HIDING!

---

*R*uth, sitting in the front seat said something about "this isn't the way to Iriga," but Aunt Olive told her she was going to go to the location the MacDonalds had picked out. Kids don't argue with grownups, and we were pretty numb by then anyway. We drove to Guinobatan and then out in the country, until by mid-morning we came to the nipa hut that Uncle Mac had selected as the gathering place. It was located near the barrio of Malabago, about 20 kilometers from Legaspi and on a secondary road that was still rather frequently traveled (see map #2). The MacDonalds, the Cooks, and Dave Martin were already there. The house, which had previously been used as a church building, didn't have much by way of furnishing, and there we all were, twelve Americans in a native hut, knowing very little about how to survive under primitive conditions. And, we were getting hungry!

We found some rice and some clay pots in the lean-to kitchen, and Dave and I set about starting fires and cooking the rice. In the Philippines you didn't buy rice nicely packaged in plastic or cellophane. Rice came from the market, where you could buy any amount you could afford and brought home in your own container. Before you cooked your rice, you first needed to go over the amount you planned to cook and then remove any stones, twigs, or even perhaps a weevil or two. The rice had to be washed three times and the proper amount of water for the portion of rice added to the pot. Dave and I had learned how to do all this, including estimating the amount of water, so for the time being we were the cooks. No measuring cups, no recipe books, just a clay pot, some rice, water (which in this nipa hut did NOT come out of a tap), some banana leaves (handy right outside the door), three stones, and some firewood.

It was a subdued bunch of people who bedded down that night in that little nipa hut. No one knew what was happening "back home" or anywhere. No lights, no radio, no newspaper— completely cut off from all we had formerly known. We hadn't heard any bombing noise at all during the day, though some of the men and boys had climbed a hill and had seen planes in the direction of Legaspi. Maybe the landing of Japanese troops was just a rumor! But, probably not!

Ruth, Dave, and I were wondering what had happened to our folks and whether we would ever see them again this side of heaven. Aunt Olive tried to comfort us, saying she would "be our mother." But, that completely turned me off, and I probably became somewhat snotty. She wasn't MY mother! Aunt Maude (Cook) was a little more cuddly, and I got along with her better. She would quietly intervene on my behalf several times over the next few weeks. The MacDonalds, with whom we felt right at home, were a big help too. Psalm 27:10 as well as Psalm 23 were of great comfort to me.

Malabago nipa hut. L–R, front row: Uncle Mac MacDonald, Helen MacDonald, Auntie Margaret MacDonald, Uncle Tom Cook, Aunt Olive Rohrbaugh, Aunt Maude Cook, David McAnlis, George MacDonald. L–R, back row: Uncle Dave Martin, Jean McAnlis, Ruth McAnlis.

A couple of days later we moved to a more secluded hut, about 200 yards off the road. The cars we had come in on December 12 were hidden in the jungle, away from prying eyes. This house, as all nipa huts, was built on stilts to keep out the damp and the creepy-crawlies. Our "facilities" were an outhouse, off to one side of the hut. I'm not certain where we got our water. During our stay of about three weeks in this house, Uncle Tom (Cook) proved to be a master entertainer, as he made flutes out of the local bamboo. We were fascinated with his careful carving, and we tooted and whistled with gusto. It took awhile for him to get the holes in just the right place to produce "music" of any sort.

Uncle Mac could do almost anything (as he proved time and again during our seven months of "freedom" in the hill country), and he was a good scrounger. He got us all settled down on mats. I can't remember if we had mosquito netting, but there didn't seem to be so many mosquitoes in the hills as in the lowland. After a couple of days he managed to achieve communication with Filipino friends, and news and visitors started to show up. Dina Cala and Drina, two women students at Albay Bible School, residents of the Visayan Islands who had been stranded in Legaspi by the landing on December 12, came to assist the mission group. They took over the cooking chores and such shopping as was needed or available. All we could pay them was their food and a place to sleep.

But, we had NEWS! Dad was still in Legaspi with his hospital, but under house arrest. Mother had gone on the bus to Iriga, and no word had yet come from her. There were lots of rumors too with each new batch of visitors. We heard that the LaPortes and Daisy Hendricks were in hiding in another area of the hills, but they did not want to join our group for they felt it was already too large and too visible. The American and British business people had also managed to escape to the hills where they were being hidden by Filipino friends. They remained in separate and isolated groupings and managed to remain hidden throughout the war.

Christmas Day 1941! Not at all what we had planned! Dad was safe but where was Mother? I'm sure small gifts (handmade) were exchanged and we kids had the gifts Mother had packed in that little suitcase. But, it was a subdued day. We took comfort in God's promises and His greatest Gift of His Son to be our Savior. We undoubtedly had a church service. I know that we had services each Sunday during our sojourn in the hills, and we invited any and all interested Filipinos in the area. We all knew many hymns by heart, and Auntie Margaret had a beautiful contralto voice to help lead the singing. Uncle Mac, who couldn't carry a tune in a bucket, nevertheless seemed always able to find exactly the right Bible reference to use for a text. Nor did the lack of commentaries and sermon helps seem to slow him down.

CHAPTER 25
MOTHER IS HERE!

Finally, on January 3, 1942, we were awakened in the middle of the night by a hubbub outside the hut. There was Mother! She was weary and foot-sore but whole in mind and spirit, with arms long enough to hold all three of us kids in a tight hug! The story of her escape from Legaspi, days in the jungles near Iriga, and her trek to rejoin us would fill a small book by itself, but I'll condense.

It seems that Dad never intended for Mother to stay with him, and so he sent her on (over protests) to Iriga, where they supposed we had been taken by Aunt Olive. Iriga is about fifty kilometers from Legaspi, so temporarily she was safe enough but had absolutely no idea where her kids were. It took several weeks, during which time the Japanese were expanding their beachhead and moving up the main road, for Filipino friends to get word to her that we were okay and were with the MacDonald group hiding near Guinobatan. She found Filipino church members who were willing to take her to her kids, but she would have to walk much of the way.

So, by back trails on foot and sometimes riding on carabaos (water buffaloes) she made her way south towards us. Finally, they came to a place where they would have to not only cross the main road, but would have to pass a checkpoint. One of the men had a car in which he was carrying abaca (pronounced "AH-bah-ca") fibre (used to manufacture hemp rope). The plan was to have Mother lie down on the floorboards, cover her with the abaca fibre, and brazen it out past the checkpoint. Anyone who knew Mother knew that her

Mother arrives! January 3, 1942. Jo McAnlis and her three kids are near the right side of the picture, next to the two Filipino men who assisted her in her journey.

nose was so sensitive that she had to use special non-allergenic face powder and that even the slightest touch to her nose often set her off on sneezing spasms that lasted through ten or twelve sneezes. And, abaca is dusty! But, there was no alternative. Putting everything into God's hands, she climbed into the car, lay down on the floorboards and was covered with abaca. All through the dusty ride, her nose acted as if it had been anesthetized, and she was brought safely through the road block and much closer to where we were hiding. She had to finish her travels on her own two feet, and when she arrived her blisters were so bad that her helpers were half carrying her.

Not too many days after Mother joined us, we were awakened in the middle of the night by Filipinos who told us that we had to move because the Japanese were coming to capture us. So, we immediately moved on to another house, farther away from the road. We followed trails in the cogon (pronounced "CO-goan") grass—very pretty in the starlight, growing six and more feet tall but with razor sharp edges on each blade of grass. Once Uncle Dave (Martin) gashed his forehead on a length of barbed wire that was strung between two trees. He couldn't see it in the dark. We took only what we could carry, though I believe we did have Filipino friends who helped with the baggage. Aunt Olive was in her 60s, but she was a game "old" lady and kept up. The Cooks, missionaries to Manchuria but sent to Legaspi to be "safe from the Japanese," were also in their 60s but very sharp and sprightly. This time we found an empty school house with real wooden floors on its upper story. We moved right in and spent ten restful days there. It was there, at Palanas, that we were close to a river. Uncle Mac often took all us kids swimming—a rare treat! You need to remember that in this whole month we had not had the privilege of running water or regular bathrooms with tubs or showers. And, it's hot in the Philippines!

We had to move once more in that first month of the war (at one time with only fifteen minutes notice—George MacDonald noting that we even left our dinner on the table). We found the place where we would "settle" for the rest of our time of freedom—in the hill country around Jovillar, near the barrio of Lilibdon. There we found a nipa hut near the top of a hill. At first we all crowded into one room, but it took almost no time at all to add a second room to the original structure so that it would accommodate thirteen Americans and their two faithful Filipina helpers.

CHAPTER 26

OUR NEW HOME IN THE HILLS

Nipa huts made of timber bamboo are notched like the logs in a log cabin, laced together with rattan, and thatched with palm fronds or other thatching. Timber bamboo grows to a diameter of four to six inches and is very sturdy. It can be split and fastened to floor cross-pieces to form a floor, which sits three or so feet above ground. That elevation provides for ventilation and keeps you up and away from snakes and such. While it is true that centipedes often inhabit thatch roofing, they usually mind their own business, and rarely drop down from their homes. We had no trouble with them.

After some months, the LaPortes and Daisy Hendricks, who were having a hard time surviving in the country, joined our group. That made too many for the main house, which by now also included a lean-to kitchen and porch. Mother had another hut built some distance away from the main house for herself and us kids and Aunt Olive. It was just big enough to hold the five of us if we lay down with the four us McAnlises side by side and Aunt Olive at our feet. We used the hut only for sleeping, or in extremely stormy conditions. Under our woven sleeping mats we placed six inches of cut grass (like hay) as a mattress—very comfortable, and we were never bothered with bugs, either. Because our hut was on stilts, as were all the houses, we placed several hen nests. Chickens are a great warning system if critters come prowling around.

How did this diverse group of missionaries and their kids manage to survive "on their own" for seven months? But, we weren't "on our own" at all. We knew our merciful God was with us, and He provided kind Christian friends, Filipino, and Chinese, who loaned money on our promissory notes so that we could buy whatever was available. That was mostly rice and some chickens and meat (pork) if the farmer had animals. There was no refrigeration, so when a farmer butchered, the word would go out, and people who wished to buy would gather round. Filipinos do not cut up a pig or chicken the way we do in the States. No steaks and roasts—just chunks hacked off the carcass with a bolo.

For Ruth's and my birthdays, Mother somehow managed to purchase a whole pig, and we were treated to lechon (pig, roasted over coals) for the whole group of Americans and the Filipinos who came to help roast the pig. Getting enough wood to make a bed of coals takes a lot of work, and turning the spit is not only hot but tedious! As I recall, our Filipino helpers stuffed the pig with onions, cooking bananas, and lemon grass. The pig cooked slowly all day, but oh, the results! Crispy, crunchy skin on the outside, and juicy tender meat on the inside. Unforgettable!

Birthday lechon. Under the mango tree near the "big house."
Ruth and Jean hold the long bamboo pole on which the pig was roasted.

Washing sweet potatoes for supper.
John and George MacDonald and Jean and David McAnlis have that chore.

We became quite proficient at living off the land. Sweet potatoes, considered by many Filipinos to be "poor people's food" were available for the digging. They grow in large patches and seem to thrive on being disturbed, since wherever a runner gets buried in the digging, new roots form at each leaf intersection and soon you have more sweet potatoes. The largest potato we dug was big enough to feed all sixteen of us for a supper. Many leaves and other plants of all sorts went into our stews. We learned the edible leaves and scoured the countryside for them.

The hill country was virgin land and very fertile. When we arrived at our last stop in January 1942, a corn crop was just at the end of its harvest. The farmers immediately stirred up the ground and planted another crop of corn. They sold us all we wanted of fresh sweet corn, though they themselves waited for it to mature and dry before they harvested it for their own use. We ate from that crop in April or so. The farmers repeated their planting once more, and in the middle of July 1942, when we were captured, we were eating from the third crop of sweet corn. Bananas and papayas were available year round. There was a mango tree near the main house, and coconuts abounded for the picking. Once we went to a place where the residents were "sugaring off" their sugar cane crop. That was an interesting process to watch from start to finish. The end result was a hard brown sugar, something like the "panoche" you can buy in specialty stores or Mexican markets.

Each member of the group had a job to do to help make our lives more comfortable. Uncle Dave headed up the wood-gathering crew, since all our cooking was over open fires. All the girls helped with food gathering and preparation. Uncle Mac took a snapshot of John, George, David, and me as we squatted around a shallow wooden basin busily washing sweet potatoes for dinner. (He took other pictures too of our life in the hills, and he thrust that camera under his mat when we were captured. Filipino friends retrieved it and kept it for him until after the war. See paragraph about pictures in Acknowledgments.)

CHAPTER 27

"NECESSITY IS THE MOTHER OF INVENTION."

I'm not sure where we obtained eating utensils, but we each had something on which to place our food. Cleaned out coconut shells make dandy bowls and scoops. David and George MacDonald had the job of keeping the water jars (large clay vessels) filled with water from the spring about half way down our hill that Uncle Mac had discovered and cleaned out. We had nothing to carry water in, so Uncle Mac devised water "tubes" made from timber bamboo lengths with all but the bottom node knocked out. The boys carried these tubes over their shoulders and dumped the water into the pots. It took lots of trips to keep us supplied with water. We all learned to be very frugal in its use. The women taught school to us kids, partly to keep us up to grade level and also to keep us busy. There was always washing and mending to do. Uncle Tom became the barber for the group, using hand clippers and barber shears obtained from who knows where. He also became the specialist at stripping abaca for use in making coarse string and rope.

Uncle Mac, after Mother allowed that she could probably make some sort of bread if she only had an oven, quarried out stones from a cliff edge. With those stones and some blue clay he found near the spring, he constructed a sort of "bee-hive" oven which proved quite successful. We hadn't realized how much we missed baked goods until we had been without them for a number of months. Mother had to adjust recipes to allow the use of rice and casava flour instead of wheat flour, but the results were more than acceptable. Uncle Mac, ingenious man that he was, even constructed a shower bath by piping water (using bamboo poles with the nodes knocked out as pipes) from the spring to a large slab of stone located at a lower elevation from the spring. With woven split bamboo walls, we had us a nice bath house with "running" water!

Our light at night came from large snail shells filled with coconut oil and with a fiber wick inserted—dim, but serviceable, and better than having to go to bed with the chickens. Often, on a moonless night, Auntie Margaret would sit outside with all us kids and teach us about the constellations. We were so far from civilization that the stars shone with great clarity.

On bright moonlit nights, when there was almost enough light to read by, we kids and Dina and Drina, along with neighbor Filipino kids, would play "tubig, tubig" (Bicol for "water, water"). We would mark out a tennis-court-size rectangle on the dirt with wide lines made by pouring water along the outline. There would be a line through the middle from one end to the other. Two more lines would be made perpendicular to the middle line. Then we chose teams. One team guarded their lines one person to each line: top, bottom, middle and the two other lines. The other team members tried to get through the court to the other side without being tagged. No problem if the line became obscured—just pour on more water!

We had few books for school, though most of us had our Bibles. However, we had only one hymnal for all of us combined to use for church services. The solution was to assign one kid each Sunday to choose the hymns for the next Sunday's service. That kid would memorize all the hymns and pass the hymnal on to the next person with the list of required hymns, and so on down the line until, on the next Sunday, everyone would know all the hymns and we could have congregational singing. It worked well, and memorizing became a very useful habit. Once in a while though, the group would surreptitiously gang up on one of the kids, agreeing to "miss" memorizing one of the hymns. On the next Sunday, all of a sudden that kid found herself (yes it happened to me!) singing a solo. In the evenings, we would often have a sing-along, with as much harmony as we could all manage. Sometimes, Dina and I would sit out under a tree, watching the moonrise, and harmonize with *Out of the Ivory*

Palaces. I still can sing either the soprano or alto on that chorus.

Some time during our stay at Palanas, I had sewn a small cloth doll. I embroidered her eyes, nose, and mouth and attached a hank of Ruth's hair. Arms and legs were sewn onto the body and were moveable. From somewhere I got enough material to decently clothe her. I seem to remember that Aunt Maude (Cook) helped with this project to keep me occupied. On our subsequent "move" in the night, the doll was left behind. But, some kind Filipino found it, wrote "McAnlis" in ink on one of the legs and returned it to me after we settled in our last hut.

Playthings of any sort were hard to come by, and I was happy to have my rag doll back. Within the week, I had caught and skinned a large field mouse or two, cured their skins, and fashioned a short fur coat and smart little fur hat for my doll. Now, what would I know about fur coats and hats, neither of which are tropical attire? But, I had fun until a neighborhood cat got a whiff of mouse skin! Then it was "good-bye" coat and hat! But, the rag doll survived, and I still have it.

We sometimes did get sick or injured during our hill-country stay. Uncle Mac bruised or broke some ribs while quarrying that stone for the oven. We bound him up tightly, and hoped for the best. We also had the occasional flu or sick stomach. One of the MacDonald boys had a bout of what we thought was rheumatic fever and was kept in bed most of the time. We "doctored" ourselves as best we could, since there was no way to get help quickly. At best, a messenger would be sent to Legaspi, but sometimes it was difficult for our Filipino friends to get back to us right away. Doctors Ago and Fontanilla did

Dad arrives! L–R: Ruth, Mother, David, Dad, and Jean beside their little nipa hut, July 2, 1942.

make trips to check out our health and prescribe within their limited resources. Medicine, along with currency, was becoming scarce. They brought news and gifts of food and some clothing.

Occasionally they brought letters from Dad. In one we learned that Dad, after being sent by the Japanese to Naga (about ninety kilometers from Legaspi) for detention with some American priests, had been liberated when the guerrillas retook the city. The Filipinos wanted him to stay with them and be their doctor, but he felt he must make every effort to get back to his family. Mostly by foot he made his way south, helped by Christian Filipinos all along the way.

At 6:50 a.m. on July 2, 1942, he appeared in our camp looking not much the worse for wear! What a joyous occasion! Our family was whole again! Aunt Olive moved into the "big" house to make room for Dad in our hut. Life went on with its unhurried pace, and I believe we began to think we might just stay in the hills of Lilibdon until war's end, whenever that might be.

CHAPTER 28
RADICAL CHANGES

But, our stay in the hills came to an abrupt end the morning of July 15, less than two weeks after Dad had joined us. It was early in the morning. I was sitting on the bench under the mango tree near the big house reading my Bible. Aunt Olive was nearby, and I think Ruth and Uncle Dave Martin were too. Suddenly, I heard a swishing sound, such as running people make when their pant-legs rub together. I looked up and saw a fixed bayonet just a few inches from my nose. The bayonet was attached to a gun, and the gun was held by a Japanese soldier. Looking beyond the bayonet, I saw a pale George MacDonald, half clothed and dripping wet, being pulled along by his arm by another Japanese soldier. George had been showering at the bathhouse down the hill when the Japanese patrol, with their Filipino guides, came along the path and captured him.

A rough gesture with the gun indicated that we were to move to our right where the rest of the missionaries, roused from sleep by the soldiers, were gathering outside the big house. They lined us up in a semicircle and placed a machine gun facing us. We had heard that the Japanese Army had set a certain time limit for "aliens" to surrender themselves and after that "enemy aliens" could face execution. So, we didn't know what was going to happen. I expect that our parents had special fears about what would happen to their teen-aged girls. I can tell you that my knees were knocking! No matter how great a person's faith, such a shock always results in the flow of adrenaline in the body, and that stuff really "shakes you up!"

We were not allowed to speak to anyone and were kept standing there for some time while the officer in charge harangued us. I had ended up standing next to Dad, and gradually it occurred to me that he was humming under his breath. Listening carefully, I could make out the tune: *His Eye is on the Sparrow, and I Know He Watches Me!* We all knew that song, every word from memory! And, what peace came over me as God's promises were renewed in my heart. My knees stopped knocking and my heart rate came back to normal. Though I did not get to walk beside Dad on our trek to the road after our capture, my sister Ruth did, and she tells me that Dad hummed that song all the way to the road. We were allowed to take very little with us from our "homes" on the hill. Mother did keep her Bible, where she had started keeping a very brief journal, using the blank paper found at the end of some of the books. There were no names since she didn't want to implicate anyone should the Japanese discover her journal. I don't remember what I brought out, perhaps the rag doll I had made myself since I still have it in my possession. I must have lost my Bible since the folks bought me a new one in Manila later that year.

Along the way we observed several things of note. One was when the Filipino who had turned us in was paid for his efforts—30 pesos, about $15.00, or less than a dollar apiece for each of the seventeen Americans! Farther down the trail, the soldiers sensed what they took for guerrilla movement on a far hill, set up a mortar, and fired several rounds in that direction. Down in one of the valleys along the way we came to a clump of timber bamboo with several young shoots showing. The soldier who spotted them must have been a city boy, for he fell to his knees and grabbed one shoot with his hands to pull it out. What he didn't know was that all new bamboo shoots are covered with a nettle-like sheath! He found out right away and was one unhappy soldier for several hours. His companions laughed at him and made jokes at his expense the rest of our trek to the main road where we waited for transportation, whether it was a bus or a truck, I don't remember, to take us to our "prison."

CHAPTER 29
CAPTIVITY IN ALBAY

*P*rison turned out to be in house #8 at Regan barracks, the old Army post. Mother wrote in her journal (written in pencil on the blank page in her Bible at the end of II Chronicles): **"We are in house #8 in Regan Barracks Legaspi guarded day and night, and not allowed to leave the house or see visitors unless brot in by the authorities. So far our only visitor has been Dr. Ago escorted by the interpreter on July 21. On July 25 the commander called and grilled us for nearly an hour. The next day Sunday, 26th, all of us except Olive and Dr. Cook (Mrs. Cook was excused in the afternoon) were compelled to pull grass around one of the barracks from 9:15 to 11:30 a.m. and 1 to 5 p.m. The next day, 27th, the men and boys were made to work cleaning grass, also the stables. The boys were let off an hour earlier than the men."**

Our food was brought to us twice a day, in large five-gallon-size tin cans. One can about half full of boiled rice and one can half full of stew made with all sorts of vegetables, familiar and unfamiliar, washed and unwashed, cooked with some meat, usually pork. It was more than all of us together could eat, and Uncle Mac and several other adults in our group wanted to tell our jailers to cut down the amount to a more reasonable size. However, Uncle Dave Martin, who had been a missionary many years in Japan, convinced them that the Japanese would take that as a sign of weakness and would reduce our rations drastically. So, we left things as they were, and made the best of the situation, eating as much as we could and saving some rice for "snacks." As usual, we slept on mats on the floor. But, now there was no thick layer of sweet grass to cushion us. We kids had no trouble with that, but older bones were not so adaptable.

Because there had been no real resistance to the Japanese invasion of Legaspi, the city and all the buildings were intact. We were sure that we would be taken to Manila but hoped to be able to see some of the mission property as we passed by on our way to Legaspi. Such was not to be. It was dark when they moved us. Again from Mother's journal (Zechariah, this time): **"Before daylight on August 3, '42, we were taken by auto bus to the breakwater, put on a small Japanese freighter and brot [sic] to Manila arriving August 6 at dawn."**

What Mother does not include is a description of our quarters, our food, and our treatment on this more than three-day trip. First, our quarters: In the fore part of the freighter was a hold that had been fixed with shelving, about chest high all around the perimeter of the hold. Under the loading hatch the space was clear. That space was our "living room" for most of the trip. Sleeping quarters were on the plank shelving. It was fairly dark and very hot in that hold. The toilets were up on the next deck and we were allowed to use them at stated times. As to meals: We were fed twice a day—in the morning, rice and sardines (canned); in the late afternoon, sardines and rice! For some reason I still enjoy both. Occasionally we were allowed up on deck. There we were exposed to Japanese off-duty soldiers and sailors who seemed to think nothing of walking around naked except for a narrow loin cloth. However, if one stood at the rail, one could enjoy the tropical scenery for the moment. I particularly remember a loading stop at the port of Masbate. I was at the rail and gasped with pleasure when I looked down. There, in unimaginably crystal-clear water, I saw school after school of tropical fish, all sizes and colors. Beautiful!

Once in a while our being on deck would inadvertently displease our captors and we would be yelled at, but mostly they left us alone in our hold. I think we had rats for company. I know we had cockroaches.

CHAPTER 30

CAPTIVITY IN MANILA

Santo Tomas Internment Camp

*T*hen, as all voyages must end, we came into Manila Bay at dawn August 6, 1942. It wasn't until late in the afternoon, however, that we were taken by bus to Santo Tomas Internment Camp (STIC). There we joined over 3,500 other civilian prisoners of various nationalities which made up the Allied nations. By then, seven months into internment, the other internees had pretty well staked out their own territories, such as they were, in the classrooms, offices, and dormitories. Some even had shanties on the commons areas. Mother, Ruth, and I were housed in the university library, a large area with many study tables. We used some of the tables as our beds. Others did the same. The men and boys were housed elsewhere, but we could be together outside during the day. STIC was crowded and noisy, a real shock to those of us used to quiet country living.

We were an added burden to the Camp administration. There had been a general "round-up" of enemy aliens (mostly missionaries in outlying stations) at the same time we were captured, and some of them were also brought to Manila at that time. So, it was with great relief that we learned of the Japanese Army Religious Section plan to move many missionaries (Protestant and Catholic) out to the mission headquarters compounds scattered throughout Manila. We were released and placed on "house arrest" on August 26, according to Mother's brief notation.

Ellinwood Compound, Malate, Manila

A rumor went around Camp that we got out because we signed an agreement to cooperate with the Japanese, but I was never personally aware of any missionary who collaborated with the enemy. Some of the mission chairmen may have signed a sort of "parole" with the Religious Section of the Imperial Nipponese Army. But, our release to our mission compounds was more a matter of the Japanese not wanting to have to provide food and housing for so many more internees. For, when we were released, so were the Japanese "released" from their responsibility to provide for us. No "enemy alien" was allowed to do gainful work, so how were we to maintain ourselves in the city? Once again, Christian friends, mostly Chinese business men, quietly advanced our mission treasurer such monies as were required, saying that they knew they would be reimbursed by the Mission Board after the war. So, now we were in the big "outside."

The Manila Times, a daily newspaper, was still being published, although now under the control of the Japanese. We became adept at "reading between the lines" when the paper reported that the Imperial Nipponese Army had "abandoned Attu Island (in the Aleutian Islands) just the way one would throw away a cigar butt." By this we understood that the Japanese had indeed captured at least one of the Aleutian Islands but that now it was back in American hands. There were, of course, ridiculous "news" stories, such as the one that claimed that a Japanese submarine had shelled Chicago! Filipinos reading this report, and not knowing U.S. geography, would take it at face value. They would become discouraged and believe that the Japanese were winning the war. We had some contact with Filipinos and were able to correct that impression with them, but there were many, many, more people who had no other source of "news." One item that caused a great flurry and much sorrow among all Filipinos was the "report" of the death of Deanna Durbin, their favorite singing movie star. No one knew until after the war that the story was a hoax.

Mother notes that our family was housed in two rooms downstairs at the back of Ellinwood Bible School. Ellinwood was a two-story, reinforced concrete building in the Malate section of Manila. It had both classrooms and dormitory rooms, with the kitchen and laundry areas downstairs toward the back. We, with the Bollman family of four who had been at the Los Baños mission station, and another couple whose son had been sent to the States

*Alien Registration, "Mickey Mouse" money put out by the Japanese,
Warning Note from Japanese officials to Alexander Christie.*

prior to the war, made up a "mess." That means we all ate together, the women taking turns to plan and prepare the meals. That took a bit of doing. We did have an older Filipino who assisted as a cook, and did most of the food shopping, since it was frowned upon to have any of us leave the compound very often. If we did go to market for food (there was little or no money for pleasure shopping), we had to wear identifying red armbands.

Once Ruth and I went for a short walk to the edge of Manila Bay to view the sunset with our mission treasurer, Alexander Christie. He had an armband, but since we were only teenagers we had not been issued any. We assumed it would be okay to go out with an adult escort who had an armband. Within twenty-four hours, Mr. Christie circulated a memo to all "messes" that he had been observed walking with two unknown aliens and had been advised by the authorities that such actions were to cease forthwith. So, we were "free" but only to a certain extent. We rejoiced in the fact that we were not behind prison fences and were not closely packed together as our friends who were in the Camp. Our lives revolved around what we could do on our own compound.

The Ellinwood Compound Organizes

There were eight eating groups or "messes" at our mission compound. In all but one (the "men's mess," those whose wives had been evacuated to the States), the women did the meal planning and part of the cooking. We McAnlis kids were always happiest the weeks that Mother was the meal planner, for then we got tasty meals and lots of variety. We didn't think the other women were so adept. Of course, there was one week, just after a heavy typhoon had caused flooding in low-lying Manila, with much loss of livestock, that fresh meat suddenly became more available in the markets. So, Dad, on his way back from clinic duty at Santo Tomas Internment Camp, brought home an abundance of fresh red meat for supper. We were enthusiastically enjoying the wonderful flavor when someone casually asked what kind of meat it was. When Dad replied, nonchalantly, that it was horse meat, a number of faces paled and forks were lowered to the table. Not much more was said at that meal. The rest of the "good buy" that Dad had found in the market was turned into sausage, heavily spiced, and stuffed into freshly laundered socks. I think the McAnlises were the only ones who enjoyed that sausage.

School took up much of our time, not only for the kids but for the teachers who were as circumscribed as we were by the lack of adequate materials for teaching. We did have some amount of paper and pencils, but books were in short supply. This, after all, had been a Bible School and did not stock books needed for elementary and high school classes. We were not free to travel just anywhere to find appropriate texts, if indeed they could be found in the city. However, that did not stop us from getting our education.

I particularly remember Miss Judson, my English Literature teacher. The books we had available were Shakespeare's *The Merchant of Venice* and Washington Irving's *The Alhambra*. I can still recite some lines from the *Merchant* with pleasure, but we spent so much time studying every detail of *The Alhambra* that I grew most disenchanted with its author, and devoutly hoped that I would never have to read anything by him again! Nor did I encounter Irving again until about twenty years later when our kids were teenagers and Bill's mother, then living with us, started reading *Knickerbocker Tales* at the supper table. I listened to a few paragraphs and then stopped her, saying, "I swore I never wanted to read or hear anything of Irving's again." Mimi showed me that the book listed no such author, but I insisted that only Irving had that style! Turns out that he did indeed write *Tales* under a pen name!

Other classes that I well remember, with a good deal of chagrin and anguish, were the math classes taught by Uncle Mac. This good man had put up with a lot from me, from the time I was little and recklessly sliding down his staircase on the abaca seat cushions (the other kids were doing it too!) and the time when, not so little, I got spooked by a water snake while swimming in the river during our "hiding out in the hills" time, and literally climbed up on him to get away from the snake! Now he had to try to cram algebra and geometry into my head. I definitely did not have a head for math, but I had to take it! I was not helped much by the fact that my two classmates were both boys who thoroughly enjoyed every problem. We had just one math book in each course. Uncle Mac had first dibs on the book and used it to prepare the lessons for the next week. We had math class five days a week. After John MacDonald and the other boy (I think his first name was Alex, but I don't remember his last name) took turns using the book to do the daily homework assigned, I got the book. It's a good thing I came last, since it often took me three hours and many tears each evening to complete the assignment. I think I passed each course, but not with flying colors!

We must have had other classes, but most remain a fuzzy memory. We did have Bible class under Mr. Christie. I particularly remember my astonishment when I found out there was at least one Presbyterian who held the a-millenial (no millenium) position in reference to the end times. Mother was staunchly pre-millennial. She would shake her head and say, "He will find out when the time comes."

We also had the advantage of continuing our music lessons. All the Presbyterian missionaries (except those few who had chosen to remain at Santo Tomas Internment Camp to work with the internees) were all on one fairly compact compound. Among that group of missionaries were lots of music teachers. Since Ellinwood Bible School had stressed music, there were plenty of practice instruments, and we kids were all encouraged to take piano and organ and voice lessons. Mrs. Bousman hosted a band practice at her house. A few of us took voice lessons. Our folks were determined that we would have a well-rounded education as well as keep up to grade level, if at all possible.

Ellinwood Compound—
Things Allowed, Things Forbidden

It must have been frustrating for the missionaries to be forbidden to go abroad to preach and teach as they had before the war. Ellinwood Church, just across the road from the mission houses, and still within the compound area, was "off limits" as far as missionaries being the actual pastors. We could attend services, however. We had a national Filipino pastor, actually a number of them over the two years we were in residence. There was already a flourishing congregation there before the war, and many of the Filipino members were still in Manila during those years, so there was always good attendance. The Japanese didn't proscribe textual preaching but did insist that nothing of a political or ideological nature would be allowed. On the rare occasions when Tom Bousman's dad preached the sermon, he was required to submit his manuscript for approval to the Religious Section of the Army by Thursday morning of the week when he would preach. A Japanese official would come to the church that Sunday and actually follow along on the printed text to be sure Tom's dad did not deviate from his prepared sermon. Japanese Army "spies" were frequently present also when our national or Filipino pastors filled the pulpit. They made no attempt to appear in any other role than censor.

I know that Ruth also used the church organ for practice, and several times she was able to play for vesper service. We were all proud of her! At times there would be church parties and gatherings, such as we had formerly had in Legaspi, and we did attend those functions.

Besides Dad, there were several other missionary doctors, Dr. J. Horton Daniels and Dr. Ted Stevenson, who had been sent for "safety" from their China mission hospitals. They were living on our compound, and they all took their turns going to Santo Tomas Internment Camp during the week to work at the Camp hospital and clinic. They also took care of our aches and pains at the mission compound where one room had been set aside as a "treatment room." You can't have that many people in a small area and not have a certain amount of sickness and accidents. In the first year at Ellinwood, Ruth, Mother and I all had dengue fever (otherwise known as "bone-break fever," since that's what it feels like) and Dad and David each had a bout of yellow jaundice. All of us recovered after weeks in bed. I believe that Dad took out Bob MacDonald's appendix sometime during our two years at Ellinwood. For surgeries and major illnesses, the Japanese permitted doctor and patient to use the facilities of the Philippine General Hospital and other Manila hospitals.

Ellinwood Compound—Special Times

Prior to the war we had always celebrated religious and national holidays, birthdays and anniversaries. During the war it seemed important to pack as many "memory builders" as possible into our lives. We especially celebrated important dates for those members of our families who were in the States. Brothers Bill and Allen were regularly remembered in this way.

Sometimes our entire compound would have a sort of "Talent Night," where various missionaries would perform a special selection. Dr. Daniels entertained and amazed us with his virtuosity on the saw! He used a plain carpenter's saw with the handle end held between his knees and the other end held in his left hand. With his right hand he used a violin bow to make music on the dull edge of the saw. It was the movements of the saw blade made with his left hand that made the different notes. The music is somewhat like that of the Hawaiian slack key.

Auntie Smith could always be counted on for several vocal solos at our Talent Nights. She conducted voice lessons for some of us, and at times we, her students, were included on the program. I remember, with a good deal of discomfort to this day, the time she slated me to sing *Would God I Were a Tender Apple Blossom*. The music was well within my range, and the tune was the familiar *Danny Boy* (or *Londonderry Air*). But the words! They had to do with some desperate, love-sick, young man wishing that he was an apple blossom so that, as a petal, he could drop softly down and nestle in the fair bosom below! Now how could a fourteen-year-old girl put any feeling into that? All I can say is that the audience was kind! Nobody snickered.

The "men's mess" was composed of missionary men whose wives and families had been sent back to the States. These men had been caught in the Philippines and now had to wait and wonder, as did their Stateside families, how their loved ones were faring. These men hired a cook to take care of their "mess" but the cook was not too familiar with American baking. I had somehow developed the knack of baking and icing cakes, adapting the recipes as various U.S. ingredients became scarce or unavailable. I made quite a number of birthday cakes for the "men's mess." They were iced too with seven-minute icing, which is about the only kind that will "set up" in the tropics. (Look in an old recipe book to see what is involved in making seven-minute icing! Remember, we didn't have electric mixers in those days!) I kept track of expenses and the men reimbursed me for the cost of materials. I never charged for the fun of baking and icing the cake.

After several of the "single" men were chosen to be among those internees repatriated on the *Gripsholm* late in 1943, the remaining members of the "men's mess" broke up the group. Uncle Albert chose to move back into Santo Tomas Internment Camp some months after that. Perhaps he hoped that being in Camp would give him a better chance for repatriation if another opportunity came along. None did, and he was in Santo Tomas until it was liberated in early February 1945.

Besides family-style celebrations and special programs, on our mission compound we instituted "fruit basket upset" Friday nights. Aunt Nell (Brown) did the planning, drawing up a schedule, and sending it to each mess once a month. There was a general "upset" of each "mess" with individuals being parceled out to other eating groups and people from those groups coming to ours. The numbers at table always stayed roughly the same, but the makeup of each group changed remarkably.

Friday nights also were game nights, so the host and hostess of each eating group had to plan not only the meal but also the parlor games that would come after the meal. Everyone was expected to participate. Since we had people varying in age from sixty+ down to small children, four years old or so, it was a challenge to make the evening interesting for all. I personally enjoyed the opportunity to interact with other than my regular "mess mates" and I believe that the idea was a sound one and helpful to our mental well-being. Did you ever try living in close quarters with many people other than your family for over two years?

But, that was just a prelude to even closer quarters!

Ellinwood Compound: The Axe Falls! July 1944

For a time, rumors had been circulating that we were going to be re-interned. I remember that Mother had been convinced from the day that we had been released to house arrest in August of 1942 that such a time would come. Other women on the compound were skeptical of her preparations and thought her foolish. But, over the months, she had quietly set aside such canned goods as she thought might keep well. These were usually canned meats and sweets, if she could find them in the market. Mother sent some of these canned goods with Dad when he went to Santo Tomas for clinic duty. There, he gave them into Uncle Albert's keeping for future use, should we be returned to Santo Tomas Internment Camp. Mother also stocked dried beans. These latter items had to be regularly sunned and checked for bugs, so she did not send any of them into Camp.

In her journal entry dated November 4, 1944, she harks back to the day of our re-internment: **"Most were shocked when the military police came about 5 p.m. July 7 to tell us to be ready to go by 9 a.m. the next morning. We packed all night. Our mess sold most of our supplies of flour and sugar after giving much away mostly to servants. We were each allowed four pieces of baggage which included our beds. Having little of household effects, we packed up all our food contrary to orders—but it was a chance to take it and a certain loss if left behind."**

Mother then inserts the comment: **"Today we are thankful for it. The October food on the line is only 880 calories per day per capita."** ("On the line" refers to our twice-a-day distribution of cooked food from the central kitchen. We all had to stand in line to receive our portion of food. Everyone kept his eyes on the server to be sure that he received an equal portion!)

When the Japanese orders for us to get ready for re-internment had come on July 7, the markets had closed and there was no way to obtain any more food. We had to take what we already had. I have a vivid memory of Mother packing the trunk we would take with us. In the bottom, a layer of clothes or bedding; then shake in a layer of dried beans and cover with the next layer of clothes. Tuck a can of corned beef down into a corner and a can of cocoa or tin of jam in another corner. Repeat layers until the trunk is full! We prayed that the Japanese wouldn't inspect too closely or would overlook the infraction of their orders.

Mother writes in her journal which she now kept in the back pages of a notebook containing recipes: **"July 8,'44 Off to Santo Tomas again. Put in the gym. Saw brother J.A. (Dad's brother, Albert) across the road while having baggage inspected."** (Mother's trunk did pass. That of a Baptist missionary, who had done essentially the same thing as Mother, was ripped to pieces and contents scattered all over the place. It seemed to depend on who was doing the inspecting. In addition, Uncle Albert had arranged to get himself included in the group internees who helped with our "processing" at Santo Tomas. Somehow, he managed to get our package of canned goods into our pile of luggage.)

Santo Tomas and Los Baños Internment Camps

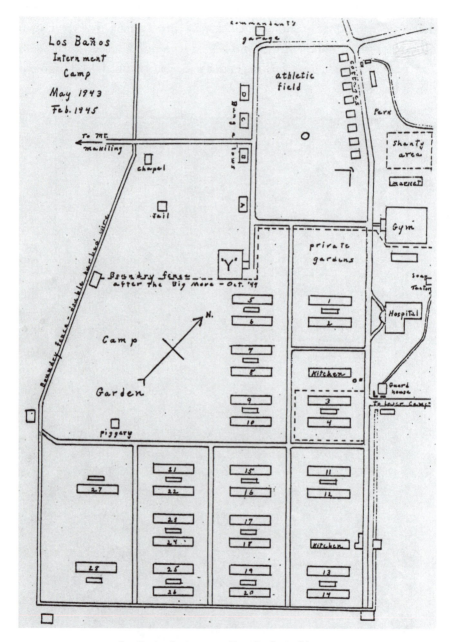

Los Baños Internment Camp's physical layout.
Jean and her family were in Barracks #17.

Signal Corp photo. In reference to Camp layout, note kitchen building in foreground.
First row of barracks: 8, 9, 10, 15. Second row of barracks: 21, 22, 23.
Third row of barracks: 27.

Floor Plan of Barracks #17 showing reorganization as the months went by. (Courtesy of Tom Bousman's journal. Used by permission.)

CHAPTER 31

CAPTIVITY AT LOS BAÑOS

Early History of Los Baños Internment Camp

*W*e were not to be at Santo Tomas very long. Mother continues: "Sunday-July 9 Left the gym between 3 and 4 a.m. by bus to Tutuban (the train station). Left 5:30 arrived Los Baños 7:30 On trucks at 9:30 for camp. By nightfall had our beds up in very comfortable barracks. Families are in #17. We rejoice to be *together*. The man in charge of us has been most courteous."

Los Baños Internment Camp had been set up in 1943, when the Japanese sent 800 men there to construct a secondary Camp, due to overcrowding in Santo Tomas. With them, they sent a medical doctor or two and the twelve Navy nurses who had been captured at Corregidor in 1942.

Los Baños Internment Camp, about forty miles south of Manila, was located on the campus of the Agricultural College of the University of the Philippines. The college grounds were about two miles from the town of Los Baños which was so named because of the hot springs in that area. Spreading north, east, and west from Los Baños was Laguna de Bay, a very large, shallow lake which reached halfway to Manila. The Agricultural College was on about sixty acres of lush, fertile land. It had quite a number of classroom buildings and dormitories. Homes for the faculty were located on the foothills of Mt. Maquiling, which rose to the west of the campus. Some of these buildings had been damaged during the fighting in 1942, but some concrete structures were still usable.

At first the internees utilized the gymnasium as headquarters. The original 800 were to prepare the Camp for further groups of internees. Filipino laborers were hired by the Japanese to construct twenty-six, barracks-type buildings, which were built in rows separated by dirt roads. A double barbed-wire fence (twenty feet or so of cleared space between the fences) surrounded the Camp. The barracks were built mostly of bamboo and nipa thatch. Outer walls and inner partitions were made of sawali, very thin (about 1/8th of an inch thick) split bamboo, woven to make sheets which were fastened to the uprights.

First Impressions

Written accounts vary as to the exact size of the barracks, and as a teenager I wasn't much interested in overall dimensions. The barracks were quite large, however, and each housed between sixty and a hundred people, depending on whose account you read. They were long rectangles, with a central hallway running the length of the building directly under the ridgepole. Running crosswise, halfway down the central hall, was another hallway which led outside either to an adjoining latrine shed or another barracks. The outside "walls" of the barracks went up about eight feet and met the rafters and thatch roof. The roof then extended even farther out to form a sort of covered veranda. Cubicles were on either side of the central hallway, onto which they opened. The interior partitions of sawali, which sided the hallways and the cubicles, went up just eight feet, and so there was lots of space between the top of the partition and the roof. Good for ventilation, but not much good for shutting out sounds from the adjoining rooms.

Cubicles, about twelve feet by twenty feet were assigned to five or six people. Fortunately our family numbered five persons, so we had a cubicle to ourselves. Couples or families with one child were permitted to put up a partition in a cubicle to form two smaller private spaces for each family. I believe that the MacDonalds, who had four children with them (Bob had been in Manila when the war started and rejoined his family when we were put under house arrest at Ellinwood), crowded into one cubicle in order to remain together.

Settling In

We were assigned to barracks #17. Several barracks in this area were built on a gradual slope. The front opened out to the dirt road (not an outside road but one within the Camp) on the east side at ground level. Farther back the floor had been dug into the gentle slope, so that our assigned cubicle, on the northeast side of the hallway intersection, was perhaps two to three feet below ground level. At the back of the barracks, the bank around the barracks was even more pronounced, and the path to the next road sloped up steeply.

Dad was resourceful, and a good scrounger too. Our guards had allowed the men to go, under guard, to some abandoned buildings and scavenge any lumber they could find and carry back. With Dad's lumber, he fashioned a loft across the long edge of the room, directly under the eaves, along the outside wall. There were no ceilings in the barracks, just rafters and thatch about twelve to fifteen feet off the dirt floor at the center of the building. So, there was plenty of room to build the loft at about seven feet above the dirt floor.

One edge of the loft met the roof where it rested on the outside wall. The loft was about four feet wide, with the inner edge overlooking our living space. So, though it was low on one side, the loft had headspace of more than four feet over the edge which overhung our cubicle. There was plenty of space for us kids to crawl along the edge of the loft to our bed mats, which were placed over a "mattress" of long grass. And, we had room to stash our few precious belongings in the space closest to the roof. We slept head to toe—Ruth in first, then Dave, and I was last up the ladder which Dad had fastened securely at one end of the loft. My head was close to the edge of our cubicle on the cross-hall. Dad and Mother had a mattress (don't ask me where it came from!) on the ground floor. No box springs, no bedstead! Over the weeks, Dad constructed a table and some benches from old planks he had found.

Our cubicle opened not only on to the hallway but also to the outside. At our part of the barracks, the dirt floor sat about two and a half feet below ground level. This "cut" continued out about six feet, almost to the roof line, and ended in a low bank. Dad put the bank to good use by devising a sort of "stove" at waist height. With a grill (don't know where it came from either) in place, it became a very well-used part of our living quarters. The veranda-like roof extended just far enough to protect the stove area from most of the rain. It must have done a good job, since I don't remember our cubicle ever being flooded, even during the occasional typhoon.

Although our two meals a day came from the central kitchen (we stood in line to get our portions), we liked to save some breakfast and, at noon, combine it with anything that came to hand from the gardens many families had started in their "backyards." Our little stove on the bank was in use most days. That way we could fool our stomachs a little bit—three meals a day!

Between every two barracks was a shed which housed showers, toilets, and a small laundry area (sinks only) for the inhabitants of the two barracks. We washed our faces, brushed our teeth and did our laundry at the outside sinks at each end of the bathhouse. The bathhouse was divided in half—one for the women and one for the men. Each half had about six toilets and maybe four showers. The showers were just pipes fastened to the uprights, with shower heads angled down toward the cement floor which had the drain. No partitions of any kind (at least at first). The toilets consisted of old-fashioned holes, six of them carved into wooden planking that was raised above a half-moon trough of metal. The whole works were on a slight incline, and the tank which held the water was at the upper end. The water supply was uncertain, at best, but when the contraption worked, the overflowing water tank was supposed to flush the contents of the trough to the lower end and on into a pit of some sort. Primitive, but workable, most of the time. You did need to be aware if you were sitting over the trough at the time the tank emptied not to be at the low end of the contraption, since, if the flow was not forceful enough, damming could occur, with unpleasant results!

It didn't take long for the women to insist on a modicum of privacy for both shower and toilet. This was especially true, since about one half of the barracks next to ours housed an order of Roman Catholic Sisters. The men were given permission to construct head-high sawali walls and a door around one shower head and also provide walls and door for privacy for one of the toilets. Any woman could utilize the privacy, but we tried to be considerate of the Sisters' needs and not monopolize the "facilities."

One Big Camp, Now!

Protestant and Catholic missionaries, over 500 in all, had been picked up by the Japanese in July 1944 when we were re-interned. All of us were taken to Los Baños. At first we were kept separate from the other 1500 or so internees who occupied the "Lower Camp." They called us the "Holy City." But, on October 7, 1944, the gate between our two Camps came down, and more than 800 disgusted residents of the Lower Camp had to move up into barracks in our part of the Camp to give the gym and other strong buildings to the Japanese. Our chosen leaders and theirs joined together to give us a strong civilian "administration" (the Executive Committee) which was able to interface with our Japanese wardens and guards. The rest of us avoided our captors whenever possible, but every day saw us bowing to a passing guard or officer. And, we couldn't avoid contact at our twice-a-day roll calls and intermittent cubicle inspections.

Hunger Sets In

We had a central kitchen where the women worked on rotation to assist the cooks to prepare such food as was given us by the Japanese. Starch was rice or cracked corn, or a mixture of the two, cooked with much more than double the normal amount of water to make it "stretch" into a viscous mush. Vegetables and meat, if any, went into a watery stew. Early in the Camp's history the Japanese had allowed a "canteen" to be set up, where those who had money or tradable items could get fruits and vegetables. Prices were very expensive, and sometime in late fall, after we had arrived at Los Baños, the Japanese shut down the canteen altogether. There was a "black market" of course, but prices were outrageous! Some of us still had a can or two of food, which we would sparingly add to our meals to make them more palatable. Mother could make a small can of corned beef last for a week! But, sometimes on very special occasions, we five would consume practically the whole can. Or, we might invite a guest or two to share the treat. Our calorie count per capita was diminishing on the whim of our supply officer, Konishi.

Few of us had salt. Sugar was unobtainable. As of November 1944, the central kitchen still had a small supply of salt, and they were careful with its use. Food was cooked in large cauldrons over wood or charcoal fires, and it was a very large job to keep a sufficient supply of firewood on hand. The men on firewood detail often used up all their day's calories in hauling wood. Malnutrition (a favorite ploy of conquerors to keep their prisoners under control) became endemic. People were starting to die daily. Over the fence that kept us in, we could see coconuts on the coconut palms, bunches of bananas hanging from the banana stalks, and papayas around their tree trunks in abundance.

After all, our Camp was on the grounds of the Agricultural College. The ground was fertile, the rainfall abundant, and produce of every kind grew in the immediate vicinity. But, we were not allowed to have any of that.

Food though wasn't the only thing we were hungry for. We longed for letters from loved ones and family at home in the States. In our entire period of captivity, we had only three brief notes—twenty-five words maximum permitted—sent via the Red Cross. Two were from Grandpa Wilson (Mother's dad) coming about a week apart in late 1944. They were not dated, so we had no idea when they were sent. They did let Mother and Dad know about the two older boys. Brother Bill, who had married after we had come back from our 1938–39 furlough, had three children, and brother Allen was well. There was other Wilson family news. Grandpa couldn't tell us, of course, that both brothers were in the Service, but it was good to know even as much as he could tell us. The other short note came from Aunt Bessie, Dad's sister-in-law. Other internees suffered the same dearth of news about their families. Our families in the States had it even worse.They received no direct word from us at all during the entire war. They were left to wait and wonder, hope and pray.

There had been one repatriation ship in 1943, the *Gripsholm*, a Swedish liner which took nine of our Presbyterian missionaries from our compound, along with a selected group from Santo Tomas Camp and from other mission compounds, home to freedom. We were not informed of the makeup of the committee who chose those who would go on the ship. We could not figure out how priority was determined. No one knew if his name was on the "list" to be repatriated until it was announced. Uncle Albert, who had been separated from his family since they had been evacuated from Korea in 1940, had hoped to be selected but was not. It was a big disappointment. He did send verbal messages back to his wife and family, which were indeed delivered. And, of course, the repatriated missionaries reported our condition to the Board, but no news after 1943.

Hope Springs Eternal

In September of 1944, I was in my Latin class (taught by a most handsome Jesuit priest, Father Sullivan) when we became aware of distant rumbling that went on and on. Sometimes it was louder, and sometimes more muffled, but we knew then that "things were happening!" We rushed outside and searched the skies toward Manila and Cavite, north of us, and were rewarded by seeing tiny specs, flying, in formation, toward the southeast. It could only be OUR bombers! We were almost free! Well, almost! At that time the Japanese had not forbidden our being outside at any time we wished.

Later, much later, we learned that this first raid that we heard was made by U. S. Navy planes. The first landing in the Philippines (Leyte) would not come for about another month. And, Luzon (our island) wouldn't see American forces landing until January 9, 1945! But, we didn't know that then! We were too excited to continue classes that day. Everybody had to get together in little groups and compare notes about just when they heard the explosions and what they sounded like and so forth and so on. Then we had to speculate on just what it all meant. We didn't have much energy for exercise or work, but how our tongues could wag!

Mother's journal skips to November 4, 1944 (her birthday) when she notes: **"Special roll call 7-8 a.m. by Japanese (farce) and inspection of baggage from 12:30 to 2:00 p.m. (perfunctory)."** These inspections became more frequent as the weeks dragged by, for by now we had heard and seen our American planes bombing distant targets. We didn't know where, but the rumors were flying. We heard "via the grapevine" that **"Nichols and Clark Fields had been destroyed; that Corregidor was bombed for hours on the 5th and 6th of November; that all Islands except Luzon were either occupied or neutralized; and only land fighting remained to be done!"** (Journal, November 9) All rumors! The Camp was alive with them.

The Japanese made many sudden inspections of the cubicles (internees all standing outside in the sun or rain, of course) to try to find the suspected radio(s) but were never successful in their searches. I never knew who had the radio, but I understand that it was completely dismantled when not in use, and the various parts were secreted by individuals within their belongings. Such American ingenuity and daring. Everyone knew what would happen if they were found out.

More rumors and reports (how quickly they spread through the Camp) were excitedly discussed toward the end of November. There had been beachheads on many Luzon points, we heard, and Manila was without light or water, with curfew from 6 to 6. Well, that is what we heard! We hoped for speedy deliverance. But, it was not yet to be.

Rations Cut AGAIN!

Meanwhile, the supplies provided by the Japanese became less and less. Konishi would tell the men of the Executive Committee who complained to him that there was nothing he could do. There simply was no more food to be found! No one believed that, although without a doubt, farming had been terribly disrupted by the war. Our "backyard" garden was beginning to produce. Mother noted that we ate our first two eggplants and some okra on November 21. On Thanksgiving day, Nov. 30, 1944, we had three small tomatoes, some mustard leaves, garlic leaves, and talinum (New Zealand spinach, and very slimy when chewed) for a salad to go with our Thanksgiving Day meal. Mother's journal records: **"Thanksgiving Day Menu 9 a.m. corn-rice mush, 25% extra portion; coffee; cocomash** (the leftover grated coconut after the milk has been squeezed out.) **At noon we fixed our extra mush with bacon and greens. 4:30 p.m. Mashed camote** (sweet potato)**, well seasoned; kidney beans with pork (soupy but good); boiled eggplant; 1 banana; 2 calamansi** (small lemons). **. . . . Opened our can of Fig Pudding saved for the occasion and at night we opened a can of corn-beef and used about ²/₃ of it."**

In December, with rations cut yet again, Los Baños Camp received another 150 internees transferred from Santo Tomas. We sent only four internees north to Santo Tomas. Mother noted in her journal that our Camp now had a population of 2146. Everyone was hungry all the time. Excluding the talk about the latest rumors, our conversation centered around food. It became common to hear grownups and kids planning entire meals that they were going to have when we were free. Brother David would talk about the meat and potatoes (or rice, because he and I both loved rice) and sauces and condiments, and he always finished his meal plans with fruit cake. Since most kids couldn't care less about fruit cake, preferring regular cake with lots of frosting, we once asked him why he chose fruit cake for his dessert. His reply: "Because it's HEAVY!"

We were getting more produce from our garden, where Dad worked diligently each day. My favorites were the sword beans—green beans, with a meaty texture and flavor, that grew more than a foot long, and were an inch or so wide. Our thoughts on food, we continued to trust that God knew our needs and would provide as He knew best. Mother records on December 14: **"Dad read for prayers the passage in Matt. About no anxious tho't for life's necessities and tonight came 2 Dutch sisters with a gift of ten salted fish and about**

2 gantas (a Filipino measure about 2 quarts to a ganta) of dry mongo beans. Truly a gift, not only from the sisters, but from God."

The Sisters, many of whom were registered nurses, really appreciated Dad and the work he did with the chronic and terminally ill internees. These ill people were housed in a barracks not far from ours and were cared for by the Sisters. Dad was the director of this hospital. Dr. Nance and the Navy nurses were responsible for the acute-care hospital, and also had more than enough work to do. It is difficult to understand how these compassionate caregivers could continue to work with the sick and dying, when they themselves were slowly starving to death. Most of the patients were suffering from beriberi, which results from lack of the B vitamins.

It was not only the amount of food rations we received under Konishi's hand but the quality of those rations—(400 grams of rice per person, per day, in September 1944, and down to 150 grams of rice in December of that year. 150 grams is about 5 ounces, or a little more than half a cup, of dry rice each per day). Polished rice is essentially pure starch with the bran and vitamins removed. (A gram of carbohydrates yields four calories so our grain ration was about 600 calories a day, divided into two meals.) We also were given some dried beans from time to time, and also some vegetables, which were always in a stew to make them stretch for the more than 2,000 people. We had almost no meat.

In the tropics, unless grains of any kind are regularly sunned and picked over, they grow their own crop of weevils and maggots. As the weeks went by, we found more and more of these little critters in our mush. At first we would pick them out, but as time passed, we just ignored them and considered them a little protein. No one in our family had ever been allowed to be a picky eater, since we were expected to eat whatever Dad served on our plates. In Camp, we didn't have the luxury of selecting what or how much food we would receive, and we continued to be "clean plate kids."

December 1944

In mid-December 1944, U.S. air activity became evident in our area again after a three-week span of silence. By now we had strict orders from our captors to stay inside whenever the planes came over. The planes were closer now, and what a thrill to peek out and see something other than the "fried egg" red sun painted on the wings. Some of the younger boys, despite the restrictions, would climb a large tree at the west end of our barracks when they heard planes in the area. Usually they were undetected by our Japanese guards, but on one occasion, David came scooting along the bank, using it for cover, and hid himself in the loft in our cubicle, just barely avoiding being caught. He was white as a sheet, and I think he kept out of that tree from then on.

Blackout conditions were enforced from 6 p.m. to 7 a.m., with only a dim electric light bulb at the hall intersection and in the latrine. Curfew was in effect from dusk to dawn. That meant no one could be outside of the barracks during those hours.

We young people often met in a vacant cubicle toward the back of our barracks in the dark hours between supper time and bedtime. Barracks #17 was a "family barracks," and there must have been a dozen or more of us from age fifteen to twenty. We talked about all sorts of things, as young people will do. During one of these sessions, I think I began to grow up. We had been discussing something, I don't remember what, when I spoke up, saying. "Well, I think . . ." and a voice came from the dark, "Jean, you don't think." Was I crushed? You bet! Set back on my heels, so to speak, I wondered: How often have I opened my mouth to express a "thought" that was vapid, or dumb, or uncalled for? But, Bob had done me a great service. Years later, in Dillon, Montana, we stopped by to see him and his family. I reminded him of what had happened that night. He, with a dry chuckle, said he remembered it well. I'm thankful for a friend who wasn't afraid to set me straight.

I had other friends in Camp too. Marita Fernandez and I became "best friends" when we were fifteen years old. Her folks, of Spanish heritage, were American citizens and were business people in Manila prior to the war. For several months I had been "seeing" a mission kid (well, he was eighteen or nineteen) from the Episcopal mission, but I broke off the relationship early in 1945 when it started to get too serious. I also met and grew very fond of two nurses from the Seventh Day Adventist Mission, whom I met at Camp. They gave me lessons in massage and frequently wrapped my wrists to relieve the pain from what the doctors called "nutritional arthritis." More likely it was neurasthenia from lack of vitamin B. Anyway, they were a comforting pair to be around and gave a further boost to my determination to become a nurse.

Christmas 1944

Christmas 1944 was our fourth since the war started. Our first war-time Christmas in 1941 occurred when we were in the hills hiding from the Japanese. We McAnlis kids had plenty to eat but didn't know the whereabouts or condition of our parents. Our second and third war-time Christmases were spent at Ellinwood Dormitory on the Manila compound. There our family was together and still adequately nourished, though under house arrest and restricted in our activities. Now, in 1944, we were starving, but we still were together as a family. Total blackouts continued, but the evening roll call was set at 9:30 for December 24, 25, and 26, so we could be out and about after dark. A bunch of mission kids sang carols around the Camp after evening chapel. Mother's journal records that the hospital patients asked for fifteen numbers ending with *God Bless America!*

Our family celebration was as near to tradition as we could make it. From somewhere I had gotten stuff to improvise a "fireplace" for our socks. I had learned to knit in Camp, and made some socks out of string—not that we kids wore either shoes or socks. Dad had found an immature betel nut frond somewhere, and we set that up on its stem end to make a small (one and a half foot) Christmas "tree." Our "mantle" was covered with greeting cards (handmade) and small gifts (also handmade) or some small treasure that had been kept all these months.

On Christmas Day itself, we had our gifts early. We had extra mush for breakfast (Mother notes: **"the nice white kind that tastes like hominy"**), and Mother gave each of us a portion of sugar, carefully kept for special occasions. After breakfast we cleaned up and started preparations for dinner. Meanwhile, Dad and Mother went around to friends and delivered a lot of verbal Christmas greetings. Mother also had a few packets of tomato seeds from our backyard garden. These went to special friends. David picked a couple of pans full of talinum (that icky New Zealand spinach) and gave away all except what was for our salad. We had plenty of sword beans and tomatoes from our garden and felt rich. Mother and Dad had invited guests for noon dinner. Aunt Olive, Alex Christie, and Dave Martin. Aunt Olive contributed a can of Spam and Dave brought more sword beans from his garden. We had had extra mush the night before, so we had enough and then some. Eight of us sat down to dinner. Mother's journal says: **"Nobody got up hungry, I'm sure.**

This was the menu served on the aluminum divided plates:

> Spam, Sword beans, boiled with the last of our bacon.
> Mush, Fried 1 square each
> Re-heated only a big bowl full
> Salad, Talinum, coconut "cottage cheese" and 2 small tomatoes
> Pudding, molded mush with sweet sauce cherry flavor
> Hot tea (no sugar)"

A word of explanation about "cottage cheese." Occasionally the central kitchen obtained mature coconuts. After the shell is broken open, the coconut "meat" is grated, and that shredded "meat" is squeezed with water to make coconut "milk," a very white, sweet but oily liquid. This was added to whatever they were cooking that day. The shredded coconut could be squeezed several more times with water, but eventually nothing more of value could be obtained. The leavings were white granular pieces, which, after a day or two, became slightly sour, and with enough imagination could be likened to "cottage cheese." Upon occasion we were served this "delicacy" from the Central Kitchen. We never had milk, much less real cheese, during our internment.

In the afternoon, after siesta time, Mother "constructed" a spice cake from leftover mush and some fresh casava flour she had traded for and almost the last of the rice flour. With it we enjoyed a can of peaches which Mother had saved since our sojourn in the hills. It had been brought to us in Manila by some church members, and Mother had kept it and put it in the trunk when she packed for Los Baños. Before cake we had a good supper of camote/carabao hash, and mongo beans with pork and greens from the Central Kitchen. (Camotes are sweet potatoes; carabaos are water buffalos, and their meat is similar to beef; the mongo beans referred to here were dried beans, of the same variety from which our present day "bean sprouts" are made). Mother opened olives to "go with" and notes that **we were all actually full, the girls to the point of discomfort.** Naturally, with our limited rations our stomachs had shrunk, so it didn't take much. Mother also wrote, **"Jean did my kitchen duty while I got dinner. That was my gift from her as she hasn't been able to use her eyes much since Dec. 1 or before."** (Due to poor nutrition and no prescription changes for my glasses in three years, I was no longer able to read or do close work.)

Farewell, 1944

The last day of 1944, about 9:00 a.m. while we were in the food line, eight of our planes appeared and strafed down near the lake, Laguna de Bay, less than two miles away. They flew right over us, and since we were in line to get our morning meal, we couldn't possibly be inside the barracks, could we? So, we feasted our eyes on this fresh evidence of American power and presence. We heard machine-gunning and more planes flew over during our morning church service. The Japanese did not stop the service, though the three-can warning signal did go up on the flag pole, and we did not tarry on our way back to the barracks.

For some reason, the rice/corn ration was increased from 150 grams to about 250 grams for the first few days of January. We did not complain! Mother noted that this rice was actually fresh and good. Rations were actually weighed out in the kitchen, so we were not "short changed" by Konishi this time!

A Special Week—January 7 to 14, 1945

Then came "Camp Freedom!" Mother records: **"Up about 1 a.m. to go to bathroom, Jean in stage whisper: 'Mother, I just overheard a guard say the Japanese have demanded all the shovels in camp immediately!' Dad, sleepily, 'Want to dig bombproof shelters.' 4:30 a.m. Dave at my bed, another whisper, 'Mother, we're to get double portions of mush . . . .' 'O.K., O.K., but don't wake me up to tell me that!'** In a few minutes a big hub-bub in 16 (barracks #16) **and a rising hum here and the NEWS broke. The Japanese had called Mr. Heichert about 4 a.m. and had him sign a receipt taking over the camp within an hour. The garrison evidently left post haste, possessions scattered, breakfast half eaten, etc. We knew the Commandant and Konishi had left yesterday in a camouflaged car, but they came back to take the others. Well the Ad. Com. was not totally unprepared and things were quickly under way. The loudspeaker in front of #15 gave directions and advice and at 6:30 a.m. there was a brief flag raising of the Stars and Stripes and the Union Jack. It was a thrilling few moments."**

Continuing on in Mother's journal: **"We've had three meals today with plenty of food—the Japanese left grain for 2 months at our *former* ration. We hit it hard today. Lots of good mush, coco mash and coffee at 8:45 a.m.**

White corn and rice mush at 12:30 and a big evening meal of beef stew with cincomas and radish, boiled camote, a few greens and dandy thick mongo beans with pork. Such food is <u>much</u> needed. The doctors say at least 80% of the camp is suffering from beriberi. I was told our mush had both sugar and tiki-tiki (rice bran) this a.m., taken from their barracks after they left. It's a crime they haven't given us such essential foods. . . . Americans man all the sentry boxes and other guard stations. Filipinos soon came bringing bananas, etc. Jean and Dad over by #14 near the fence came home with half a pomelo (like a large grapefruit) and an egg.

"A radio was soon hooked up and we've had the thrill of hearing 'This is the United States of America, Station KGEX from 6 to 9 p.m. The wonder to me is that we are free (so called) when we are still bombing Japanese bases, etc, all over the Islands according to this news broadcast. The war is far from won on any front. But, it is wonderful to hear first hand news after more than three years."

What rejoicing and excitement and thankfulness that day! We were too stirred up to settle down to anything! School sessions had stopped before Christmas, teachers and students alike too weakened by starvation to concentrate on studies. We did lots of talking, lots of listening, and lots of eating! Thank goodness that the kitchen staff kept to their stations! The Camp Executive Committee cautioned all internees to remain within the Camp for their own safety, since no one knew the conditions on the outside. It was also suggested that we should stay together so that our American forces could more easily move us out when they came to rescue us. (We had never doubted that MacArthur would keep his "I shall return!" promise.) Most agreed with this advice, but many men, especially the young, single fellows, went outside the fences. Our family did not.

We woke up the next morning (January 8) to find Japanese guards on duty once more but not the same guards we'd had before. These were Military Police, and as Mother said, **"a befuddled outfit even having to ask for food from our kitchen."** They did not interfere with any activity in Camp, and Filipinos continued to bring in food. They came to the main gate, where American, as well as the Japanese Military Police were on duty. The Executive Committee, following the pattern set early in the war at Santo Tomas Internment Camp, contracted with town and college authorities through Red Cross credit (to be repaid after the war) for food supplies. This included plenty of meat, especially beef. We looked at this bounty as truly "manna in the wilderness." In the following days, our Camp Committee, opening up the food storage sheds, found an abundance of supplies. They decided to issue each internee 5 kilos (about 11 pounds) of rice and a portion of salt, "just in case." It was a wise move!

During the week there was much American activity in the air, and we both saw and heard the planes and their destructive loads! Our spirits soared! Surely our rescue would be soon! Increased food gave us more energy. Dave and some of his friends again climbed the large tree at one end of our barracks to get a better view of the planes and their objectives. We walked with more vigor and began to hear laughter once more.

Surprise!

Then, on Saturday, January 13, 1945, in the middle of the night, we heard a voice at the crossroads of our barracks: "Important announcement! Konishi, the Commandant and his staff have just returned. Stay in your barracks until 6 o'clock." Such a buzzing in the barracks, but we finally settled down. Nothing else to do. As Mother wrote later in the day: **"At least we've had several days of better food—some real news regarding our forces."**

In the morning, we learned what Konishi's return meant—back to two meals a day and reduced rations. The first action Konishi took was to seal the kitchen and other food stores. The Japanese took the three hindquarters of beef which were intended for our supper and gave us the leavings to put in that night's stew. The "strange interlude" was over. That noon we did cook some of the rice we had been issued and that, combined with sword beans from our garden, satisfied our appetites for the time being. We still had some of the fruit and coconuts we had gotten at the gate during "Freedom Week," mostly by barter, trading our ration of cigars and cigarettes, which we had kept strictly for trading.

It's Getting Tougher!

Suddenly, without any reason we could know, American air activity, at least in our vicinity, stopped for days. Our spirits drooped! We could hear heavy bombardment to the north and could see the flames reflected in the clouds at night. We assumed that the battle for Manila was in progress. We could not know that most of the flames were from fires set by the Japanese and that in the battle for Manila over 100,000 Filipino civilians would die. During our "Freedom Week" we had heard for ourselves on the radio about the landing at Lingayen Gulf, north of Manila. But, with the return of Konishi and the Commandant, we were back to garbled "news" quietly passed on from the clandestine radio reports.

Mother's journal (now in her cookbook, not her Bible) stops after her recording of Konishi's return on January 14. I think she simply ran out of paper to write on, since her entire notebook was filled. Evidently we had no other paper. So, the account of those last five weeks before our rescue comes from my memories and from recollections of other internees who wrote about their war experiences.

We now had more frequent roll calls. Blackouts and curfew were strictly enforced. Food rations dropped drastically, with supplies consisting of old rice which was infested with weevils. Severe penalties were threatened for those who continued to slip out of the Camp at night, though there were some who still dared. Twice, during these weeks, the Japanese did catch men who were either going out or coming back into Camp through the fences. In each case, the men were executed. One was wounded and left to lie until Konishi felt like taking the time to order his death. Camp doctors begged to be allowed to minister to the man, but permission was refused.

The monotonous weeks dragged on. All of us were starving, and many were in the hospital with beriberi symptoms so severe that they were even too weak to get to the food lines. Dad was more than busy in the chronic ward. After my sixteenth birthday, February 1, I was allowed to assist the Sisters caring for the patients. With advanced beriberi (so-called "wet" beriberi), fluid fills the intracellular spaces to such an extent that the legs swell to gargantuan size, and the skin splits and oozes, somewhat like tree bark in the spring, when the sap rises. This fluid is found in and affects all parts of the body, including the brain. I remember my first time at the hospital when Sister assigned me to feed thin gruel to a man whose legs resembled tree trunks. She said, "Now, don't worry if he tells you that the moon is made of green cheese." He had completely lost his mind along with his physical health.

I knew that Dad had spent time begging the Japanese authorities for even the silk from the fresh corn that they ate so that he could steep it in water and perhaps have some vitamins to "treat" his patients with. They wouldn't give him even that. We had no medicines for our patients, but what they needed was nutritious food. Now it was too late. Many died. The doctors wrote "beri-beri due to starvation" on the death certificates. The Camp Committee had more and more trouble finding able-bodied men to dig the graves. Two Presbyterian missionaries, Dr. Magill and Rev. Blair died of beriberi; one on February 19 and the other on February 20 of 1945.

Happy Birthday, Jean

For my sixteenth birthday, February 1, 1945, Mother had hand-embroidered a bath towel, with the date and L.B.I.C. embroidered on one end. She also presented me with an autograph book (they used to be very "in" when I was a kid) made from an old address book which she covered with material to make it stronger, and also, I suspect, to make it less obvious to any Japanese "inspectors." She had asked quite a few fellow internees to write greetings and wishes in the book. Lots of them included favorite recipes with their notes.

Our clothing was in a sad state. Mother had one dress. Ruth and I were about in the same straits. Dad had one or two shirts, which we tried to keep as neat as possible, since he wore a shirt each time he visited the chronic ward where the Catholic Sisters were the nurses. (That was a source of real gratification to them, since it helped to maintain their modesty as well as kept up the appearance of professionalism.) Underclothes were threadbare at best. Our clothing had been mended and patched without end. Perspiration takes its toll on cloth, and most of us had no soap to use for laundry purposes. We had long since exhausted our supplies of almost everything needed for normal daily living. We hadn't had toothpaste for months, though we did still have our old toothbrushes and used them with water. Salt, when we had it, was for flavoring our bland food and to replenish what we had sweated off during the hot days. Keeping clean became a real problem, especially with the uncertain water supply. As a result, many internees contracted boils and other severely painful skin diseases.

Bright Spots

One day a group of us were allowed to go under guard to the nearby river to wash our clothes. We took advantage of washing ourselves too, the guard being young and lenient. Then, using sign language, we asked permission for David to climb a santol (fruit) tree that was near the river. The guard signaled "yes" and Dave shinnied up that tree in no time at all. He threw down ripe santols to our waiting hands, and we eagerly ate the fruit. Glancing at the guard, I noticed that he looked sad and lonely, so I took a couple of santol over to him. He bowed and hissed through his teeth, and I thought nothing more of it. Several days later, as I was on courier duty (all messages from the Camp Committee were hand carried), up in a more remote area of Camp, I heard someone behind me, riding a bicycle. Only the guards had bicycles, and I was frightened—all alone with a Japanese guard. Nowhere to run, I stopped. He drew up in front of me and got off his bike. It was the guard who had accompanied us to the river, and I relaxed a little. With a smile and a bow, he gave me a small package, returned to his bike, and pedaled away. After completing my job, I opened the package to find a small bar of soap! Cashmere Bouquet, as I recall, and priceless! A real kindness to a prisoner.

A couple of other instances of kindness are reported in books and articles I've read. John MacDonald tells of a time, shortly after we had been captured by the Japanese in July of 1942. We were housed in one of the military cottages near Legaspi, confined to the house except when forced to pull weeds for our captors, eating such food as we were given, and sleeping on the floor. There were sixteen of us, six kids and teenagers, the others being our parents or other missionaries. Each family group slept under one mosquito net at night. I don't remember how the couples and single missionaries arranged it so that they had the protection of a mosquito net.

John tells of one Japanese officer who tried out his English on us. He asked the kids if they liked to play games. I'm sure we said yes! Being cooped up in a smallish house all day for days on end without anything to do, read or listen to, was wearing. (Do I hear today's teenager saying, "Boring!")? That night, when all of us were under our mosquito nets, we heard the clumping of a soldier's boots coming toward them. It was pitch black, and no one knew what was going to happen. The clumping sound headed toward where the MacDonalds were all huddled under their net. Suddenly the edge of the net was lifted and the officer, the one who knew English, shoved in a box of double six dominos. Not a word was spoken then, but we were all grateful for this kindness and enjoyed many hours of playing dominos.

At Los Baños, a guard who loved classical music chanced to hear one of the internees, Grace Nash, who before the war had played with the Manila Symphony Orchestra, practicing violin. He came to listen as often as he could when she and her accompanist prepared for a concert. He offered to purchase food for her and her family if she would give him something to be used in trade. She gave him her remaining jewelry, fountain pens, and hoped! It was shortly before the events of "Freedom Week" and rations were very slim. Grace and her husband had three small children. On that January night when the Japanese garrison left in such a hurry, the food that this "classical music lover" had purchased was delivered surreptitiously to an internee friend of Grace's. Despite the curfew, this friend of the family managed to slip over to their barracks and deliver what had been promised.

The Battle Rages

As the American forces continued to gain ground on Luzon, our captors became more and more edgy and frustrated. Konishi seemed to reduce our rations with each American advance. We had no real news about our fellow internees at Santo Tomas Camp in Manila, but we could guess that much of the fighting in late January and into February was in that area. We didn't know for sure that they had been rescued yet, though we hoped so, and that our turn was next. Santo Tomas was freed on February 3, by a lightning strike of the 1ˢᵗ Cavalry. The city of Manila, which MacArthur had declared an "open city" late in 1941, had been spared general destruction then. Now, in January of 1945 it became a battleground when the officer in charge either did not receive or refused to heed General Yamashita's instructions to withdraw from Manila, leaving it an "open city." This officer decided to fight to the last man. Death and destruction in the city was terrible. Some historians record that over 150,000 Filipino civilians were killed. Observers, after the war, said that Manila received as much damage and destruction as Warsaw.

Some of our young men were still managing to escape the Camp at night, though they had to be back in time for morning roll call. Missing persons were a hazard to the well-being of the entire Camp. Japanese tempers were short. Among the internees there was quiet talk of how these men had contacted guerilla forces. We heard, though we never saw for ourselves, that some American dimes and some American cigarettes, had been seen in Camp. Spirits soared, then plummeted, depending on the "news." We also heard rumors that the Japanese were planning to machine-gun the internees rather than let them be rescued. We kept quiet about that, and prayed on.

By the third week in February 1945, our energy was at such low levels that most of us lay around all day except when we had to stand for roll call, food line, or to go to the bathroom. Most women had not menstruated for several months, probably a very good thing! People still got sick. Auntie Smith had a bout of bacillary dysentery early in February, but there was still enough serum to cure her disease. She wrote in a letter later that month, after liberation, that she had weighed 99 pounds when she left the hospital on February 7. Mother, in a letter after our February 23 liberation, writes that David had lost thirteen pounds since December. And, he was a fourteen-year-old boy! Dad was down to 115 pounds from his normal 135–140. I don't know how those internees who were responsible for the Camp cooking were able to keep going. I imagine that workers got a little extra ration, only reasonable, as they were doing physical labor but the kind and quality of the food was unimaginable. People were eating almost anything they could find. I know that I did eat rat and snake (not many left in Camp, and pretty slim pickings if you did catch one!), and Uncle Mac managed to down some slugs (plentiful in the tropics) after "frying" them in cold cream. We had no oil, of course. Some people tried to eat banana skins after they had consumed their last bananas. Pretty awful taste!

It Gets Worse

Then, the last straw! Konishi issued a rice ration for one week to each internee. However, this rice was still in its husk. We call that *palay* (pronounced "pah LIE") in the Philippines. It is difficult to process into edible rice under the best circumstances. Filipinos with no access to modern mills use a large wooden mortar (hollowed out from a log) and pestle to pound the rice. Once the husk is loosened or off, the rice has to be winnowed to remove the inedible parts. We had no way of processing our palay except by rubbing it between our hands. Trying to eat it, even boiled, with the husk on would result in intestinal perforation! Konishi closed the Central Kitchen, and we were left to our own devices when it came to meals. Some internees had saved a bit of the rations the Camp Committee had issued, "just in case." We all laboriously tried to grind the palay to get at the rice. Someone estimated that it used more calories to process the palay than we got from eating the resulting rice.

Rumors—or were they more than rumors?—came on Thursday, February 22, 1945, that Friday and Saturday would be critical days. American planes bombed and strafed locations very close to Camp. Of course, we were all inside the barracks and couldn't see anything, but we heard the thuds and explosions. We waited and wondered. It was that Thursday afternoon that Mother planted peanuts in our garden, about a cupful of raw nuts saved from a small crop we had harvested some time before. Dave badly wanted to eat those peanuts, but Mother always thought ahead! We might need that next crop. Who knew how much longer we would be in Camp

Let Freedom Ring!

The rising bell for roll call sounded as usual at 6:45 a.m. on Friday, February 23. I was already up and ready, so I wandered on down the hallway to the front entrance, which faced east. All internees were required to stand in front of the barracks at each roll call for an actual counting of noses. You couldn't "cover" for someone who was missing. If anybody was sick and in bed, it could be reported, but usually a guard would check to be sure.

Quite a number of us were already out in front, discussing the strange sounds we had heard in the early morning hours. It was a sort of grinding, heavy machinery or engine noise coming from the north. We'd never heard anything like that before. But, it had stopped before 6:00 a.m. and we were just mildly curious. Then we heard another sound with which we were more familiar—planes! Big ones, from the sound of it, and approaching from the north rather slowly. Certainly not the fighter planes we had heard yesterday. Now we could see them—nine big, fat planes flying in three v-shaped formations at a very low altitude. What now? Were they going to drop propaganda leaflets? We couldn't make any sense of it all.

On they came, just above the tree tops, at an altitude of 400 or 500 feet. At almost precisely 7:00 a.m. the planes were due east of the Camp. All of a sudden, from their open right-side doors came a lot of bundles. As we watched with open mouths these bundles loosed their parachutes, and there dangling from the 'chutes were men! Our men! And, that was the signal! From the other three sides of Camp (north, west and south) came the sound of guns firing, as the combined force of Filipino guerrillas and American paratroopers stormed the fences.

I turned around and raced down the central hallway towards our cubicle. Tom Bousman, who had also seen the paratroopers drop, was running just as fast down the cross hallway. We ran smack into each other, picked ourselves up, and continued running. Mother, Ruth, and Dave were in the cubicle we called home, but Dad was nowhere to be seen. We upended the table next to the interior wall and crouched beside it, pulling the folks' mattress and pillows over us. We heard the whine of bullets, but none seemed to come our way. But, we were worried about Dad. Where was he? In the midst of a flurry of firing, in he walked, cool as a cucumber! He had been out at the wash house, shaving, and had seen no reason not to finish his morning ablutions!

With his coming, although we could still hear frequent shots, we hesitantly left our position on the floor. Dad and I went out to the dirt bank near the stove to see what we could see. Shortly thereafter, we heard a booming American voice shouting, "Everybody out front and down to the playing field!" We turned around to see a young trooper, in camouflage clothing and a helmet that completely covered his head except for his face. The last American soldiers we had seen (except for the P.O.W.'s in Manila during the war) had been in 1941, and at that time they were still using the old WWI type of helmet. "Five minutes!" he called. "Just what you can carry!" And, he pulled back out of our doorway to repeat his warning at the next cubicle. David turned to Mother and exclaimed, "See, Mom! I TOLD you we should eat those peanuts!"

Rescue

Rapture! Thrills! Excitement! Thankfulness! Exhilaration! What a mixture of emotions, all positive! Weak from starvation as we were, we scurried around gathering things we thought we must take with us. We shuffled down the road with a jumbled assortment of "things." The soldiers must have thought we were mad! And, perhaps there was a little madness too! It was so sudden, and so quick! Our legs trembled and our knees shook, not just from hunger and starvation but also from some fear, for we were still hearing occasional guns firing. Crowds of internees clogged the road. We five stuck together like glue. Dad shepherded us all together as we made our way toward the playing field in the lower Camp.

There we found out what had made all that heavy engine noise during the night. While we were sleeping, or trying to sleep, part of the Airborne Battalion was headed toward Los Baños in amtracs, large vehicles, with tracks instead of wheels, and capable of moving across water as well as land. They came across Laguna de Bay, that large shallow lake lying between us and Manila. Coming by water, they had avoided going through Japanese lines. (Another part of the battalion was trying to reach us by road but were running into heavy resistance by the Japanese.)

At the time of our rescue, our Camp was at least twenty-five miles behind enemy lines, and it was known that there were many Japanese troops within several hours march of the Camp. The Filipino guerrilla forces and the soldiers with them had infiltrated through Japanese lines to reach the borders of our Camp in the early hours of the morning. There they waited until they could coordinate with the paratroopers. Information about the Japanese customary exercise hour and the exact location of each guard station had been brought to American forces by some of our fellow internees who had escaped Camp under cover of darkness several weeks before. They had been helped by the Filipino guerrilla forces to reach MacArthur's army. These men let those in charge of our rescue know how many internees there were and their physical condition. And, they had also brought word that there was strong reason to believe that our Camp was scheduled for massacre on the morning of February 23. The American Army was also well aware of the recent massacre of more than 150 American P.O.W.'s on the island of Palawan when the Japanese mistakenly assumed that our forces were headed their way. The pressure was on to plan and coordinate the rescue raid.

And, it was magnificently done! God was truly watching over soldiers and internees, as many, including General MacArthur, declared. In the diversionary force approaching from the north by land, two Americans were killed by dug-in Japanese forces. Not one American soldier lost his life in the actual raid. One internee took a bullet in his arm. None of the other internees suffered more than a minor burn or so from a close miss or a spent hot shell. One Filipino guerrilla was killed in the Los Baños raid firefight.

Speaking of fire, some internees were so confused by their sudden rescue that they milled around and did not follow directions. In fact, things were chaotic for a number of minutes. Some people even refused to leave their barracks, or else they wanted to bring along everything they had—ragged clothes, precious old magazines, old tin eating equipment, leftover food, whatever. The paratroopers finally had to resort to setting the barracks on fire to get some of the people out and moving. The bamboo and thatch barracks were, of course, prime fuel and blazed away furiously.

There were already lots of internees at the playing field, milling around the amtracs which were parked there. The drivers let down the ramps and we piled aboard, squeezing in as many as we could. The soldiers were grinning and reaching out to anybody they could. Some of them gave candy and their own rations to the internees, but I don't recall too much of that going on. It seems that the Army's experiences when they released the Santo Tomas Camp internees on February 3 had been impressed on these soldiers' minds. There, at Santo Tomas, several of the internees died from overeating rich food on the day of their release. These guys weren't going to have us repeat that mistake.

"Through Fire and Through Water" (Psalm 66:12)

Amtracs are open to the sky. Their sides are double walled, with about a foot of storage space between the walls. A machine gun is mounted at the front near the driver and is manned by an ever-watchful soldier. As we rumbled down the road toward the lake, we felt perfectly safe now that we were with Americans and protected by those thick walls. However, there was sporadic sniping by the Japanese, and before our amtrac got to the water, while passing through a coconut grove, the Japanese opened up on us too. Some of the men and boys had been sitting on top of the side walls. They jumped down in a hurry, never mind that they sort of squashed some of us. We were all crouching on the floor of the amtrac. Looking up, I watched as the gunner matter-of-factly swung his machine gun around and took care of the problem, reassuring us with a shake of the head and a muttered "it's nothing!" Several amtracs in our group were in the same incident, and all gave answering fire. We did hear later that one amtrac did take direct hits, with three people being slightly wounded.

During our ride across the lake (see map #3), a line of amtracs, more than fifty of them, was strung out over the waters, almost as far as we could see. Our amtrac was about in the middle of the line, so we had a good view. American planes were overhead to discourage Japanese fire, but the Japanese had nothing that could reach us out on the water. We were within our own American lines when we came to shore.

We were only the first group to be brought out. There were more than 2100 internees plus all the soldiers involved in the rescue. About 1500 internees came out on the "first wave." The amtracs had to return to pick up the rest of the internees, who by that time had walked the two miles to the shore and were waiting, with a good deal of anxiety. The Japanese were starting to close in on the little enclave. The paratroopers who had come in the first wave of amtracs had brought howitzers and kept the Japanese forces well away. I have read somewhere that some of the amtracs had to make a third trip to complete the evacuation. By then the Japanese guns were starting to get the range, and things were getting dicey. Later we heard, to our great sorrow, that after our evacuation, the Japanese soldiers had vented their sadistic rage on the innocent residents of Los Baños. Within the week, there had been wholesale massacre and many atrocities.

At Mamatid (see map #3), internees mingle with the G.I.s who had rescued them.
Note the amtracs (with machine guns) drawn up on the beach
just behind the line of army trucks. (Signal Corp photo.)

"Into a Wealthy Place" (Psalm 66:12)

On the beach where the amtracs debarked us, a field kitchen had been set up to feed the men who were our rescuers. We sniffed hungrily at the wonderful odors of fresh bread! We sat around for awhile, but soon trucks arrived to take us to, of all places, prison! It was Muntinglupa, the federal penitentiary which was about twenty miles south of Manila. It had been captured by American forces just a few days before we were brought there and was the only safe place the Army had to put the more than 2100 of us. It provided housing for all of us, plus many G.I.'s (a new term we quickly picked up). Some of us slept on the floor that night, but by the second night all had cots to sleep on. We didn't mind this "prison." We felt safe, though we could hear big guns firing most of the night, and several times had "red alert" scares.

After paratroopers land at Los Baños to free POWs they are supplied by air with material to block Jap attacks.

NEWSMAP

SOUTHWEST PACIFIC

Vol. 3, No. 13 — 0 MAR. 1945

The first weeks, supplies were dropped by parachute into the prison grounds. The area around Muntinglupa was still being contested.

An Army field hospital was functioning at Muntinglupa, and our sick and wounded were taken there. The doctors and nurses were thrilled to treat more than just war wounds! And, three days after we were released, they had a real change of pace, as they delivered a baby for one of the internees. It may be that the medical staff also oversaw the pace of our feeding, for we were started out very gradually, with small amounts of nourishing food. There was quite a bit of grumbling, but when the story of what had happened at Santo Tomas got around, everybody settled down!

The McAnlis family in Chow Line at Muntinglupa, March 1945

Within the week, we were on full rations and how we enjoyed them. Of course, we had to stand in line to get our food, but then we had lots of practice doing that! In this line you could have all you wanted, and the cooks were more than generous. If you wished, you could have five or six TABLE-SPOONS of white sugar on your cereal in the morning! We didn't want it all dumped on our cereal, but when we held out an empty container, the cooks cheerfully spooned in the rest of the sugar. With five of us in our family, whenever we did that we ended up with twenty-five tablespoons of sugar to use for something else. And, internees had learned to be inventive, if nothing else.

At two tablespoons of sugar to one ounce, we had at least twelve ounces, or one and a half cups of extra sugar every morning, if we wished. Save that up a day or two, add a few tropical chocolate bars (very concentrated, and generous sized), pour in a little milk (also saved from the food line) and with very little trouble, you could come up with a batch of marvelous fudge! At least we thought it was good! We used our Army mess gear as containers to boil up the candy.

News from "Home" (The States)

Besides the nourishing and tasty food for our bodies, we were reveling in all the letters from "home" that were awaiting us at Muntinglupa. They came via the Red Cross. We had more than three years of news to catch up on! Mother said of these letters, "It is a feast of good news." And, happy day, we were able to write letters home too. Just one letter per internee family on the first mail to go out. After all, there was still a war on. So, Mother wrote a "round robin," asking her folks to pass on the news.

My former English Lit teacher, Miss Judson, a former missionary in China, who had been sent to the Philippines to be "safe," had been repatriated to the States on the *Gripsholm* in 1943. She was living in Pasadena, California, where Mother's parents, as well as Uncle Albert's wife and family, also lived. Upon hearing of our rescue, undoubtedly from our relatives, she put it all in poetic form and entitled it "Los Baños Rescue." Miss Judson had never seen Los Baños Camp, nor suffered the severe starvation, but she captured the essence. She sent the poem, with original art work, to us after we had arrived back in America. I give it to you here, as it truly expresses the event and our feelings so well.

LOS BAÑOS RESCUE

Under the blue Los Baños sky,
Hundreds, not knowing, doomed to die;
Lying down with a sigh and a prayer –
Where were their rescuers, Oh, Where?

Dawn of another hungry day,
To endless roll-call on the way –
Sudden . . . a wild, ecstatic cry,
As against the sunrise, out of the sky
Paratroopers came floating down.
Never an angel with starry crown
Could look more sweet to weary eyes,
Than those khaki angels from out of the skies.
Nor could weary ears hear a more glorious din
Than the noise of those "amtracs" rolling in.
'Twas the sign, and without a second's delay
Philippine brothers leaped to the fray;
Crack of rifles and fearsome shout,
Bullets whistling all about,
Frantic dash of their captor's feet, —
But death was their lot in swift defeat.

Love and honor to those who died,
That a desperate need might be supplied,
And to every soldier who risked or gave
Life-blood, his fellow men to save.
(Loving Christ, when the goal was won,
Did you smile and whisper a soft "Well done?"
Did each man feel round his shoulders warm
The approving pressure of Thy strong arm?)
Joyous volumes of grateful prayer
Followed the good news everywhere,
From hearts at home that had waited long,
Filled at last with rapturous song.

Bless then, Christ! We can ne'er repay
The debt we owe for their deed that day;
Down the ages hearts ever will thrill again
To that miracle rescue by brave, brave men,
By God, Who had answered once again.
—Marjorie M. Judson

The Los Baños Rescue was not an important event in the "big picture" of war. Many history books carry our "story" as a brief footnote. In some history books, our rescue is not mentioned at all, for on the same day of the Los Baños rescue, February 23, 1945, the Marines raised the American flag on Mount Suribachi on Iwo Jima. The battle to recapture the island of Corregidor was raging as well. And, of course, in Europe the Allied spring offensive to the Rhine was starting. But, for us internees, and perhaps for our rescuers, February 23, 1945, was probably the most memorable day of our lives.

Interlude

At Muntinglupa, we were being processed for our return to our various countries. We all needed booster shots for typhoid and cholera, and we had various other inoculations too. We were measured for clothing which would keep us warm in the temperate climate of our homeland. I can't even remember all the material things that came our way via the Red Cross and the Army. I know that the coat I eventually got was a WAC (Women's Army Corp) uniform jacket. Others were similarly outfitted. Processing tried our patience, but we didn't complain. We knew we were going home. Meanwhile, there was all that good food, three times a day.

And, in the evening, every "girl" from eight to eighty, could, if she chose, sit under the stars with a G.I. (or two or three) and watch a movie on an outdoor screen. I remember one night when it seemed that the officers had pulled rank and "dated" every lady around for the evening movie. The G.I.'s were not happy! Suddenly, just after the movie had started, we heard a loud explosion outside the perimeter wall. The machine guns in the guard towers opened up with everything! We could see tracer bullets streaking orange/red toward the area of trouble. The loudspeaker blared, "Condition Red! Condition Red!" while our escorts jumped to their feet and took off running to their assigned posts. The lights all went out and the movie screen went blank. We "girls" sat there on the ground, wondering what was happening. The firing stopped abruptly.

Then, somebody came and sat down quietly by me, and more somebodies by my friends, and so on all over the field. A light or two came back on, and when we looked around, there were the G.I.'s, grinning widely, seated at our sides. All over the area, G.I.'s had taken a place at the side of every woman there, and when the officers came back from their outfits, well too bad! We finished viewing the movie with our new escorts.

Surprise!

Most of our days were pretty monotonous as we waited for transport to be arranged. One major, unforgettable event did brighten the day (and even longer) for the McAnlises. Toward the end of March 1945, or perhaps very early April, Uncle Roy (Brown) had driven to Manila with an Army chaplain, to try to assess damage to the Presbyterian mission compound. He had returned late in the day and was walking down the main "street" toward our living quarters when I chanced to meet him as I was going the other way. He had a G.I. with him and they were talking. I gave him a glance, since not too many missionaries got to be very well acquainted with G.I.'s. However, I didn't give it much thought, since we were surrounded with Army personnel of every sort. Uncle Roy stopped me and said, "Jean, I'd like to you meet a friend of mine..." and I stuck out my hand for a polite "How-do-you-do?" greeting.

This G.I. was as tall as Uncle Roy, and probably I didn't even quite look full into his face. But then, something seemed funny to me. Uncle Roy was having a hard time suppressing a guffaw, and the G.I. seemed to be half-way between strangled laughter and tears. I looked again, and suddenly, right there in the middle of the street, I threw myself into his arms and hugged him for all I was worth! It was my brother, Allen! We had heard from family letters that he was in the Army and was "somewhere" in Iran, near Russia. Never mind how he had gotten here (a short story by itself) but here he was! I was beside myself with joy. It had been six years since I had last seen him, and I had been only ten years old at that time, so it was no wonder I didn't recognize him at first. But, could we pull the trick on the rest of the family?

We continued to walk toward our living quarters, hoping to catch Mother

Above: Allen and all of us.

*Left: Allen with Ruth,
David, and Jean.*

first. But, guess what? She knew something was up! It seems that some dear Catholic Sisters had viewed my unseemly (to them) actions with a G.I. on the main street and they had hurried to let Mother know that she needed to talk to her daughter. It was only a couple of blocks, but they beat us to it. Mother was expecting some sort of surprise, though she never expected Allen! So, it was a semi-surprise. However, we were able to pull the same stunt on Dad for which he had a hard time forgiving us. He didn't recognize Allen either, when Uncle Roy "introduced" his friend! Dave and Ruth soon came on the happy scene, and what a reunion we had!

We got to see Allen a few more times before we were shipped out. He, of course, stayed with his assigned unit, and came home to be discharged after the war ended.

On Our Way at Last!

Early in April 1945, word came to get ready to be moved to Manila for embarkation and the trip back to the States. We could only gaze with shock and horror as we passed what was left of that city after the fierce fighting to retake it from the Japanese. Then it was behind us, and we boarded the troop ship, *SS Admiral Eberle*, a Coast Guard ship. The *Admiral Eberle* was a large troop transport, over 800 feet long, and this was her maiden voyage. There must have been at least three thousand former internees, though some from both Santo Tomas and Los Baños Camps had already started home on other transports. Besides the crew and the internees, the ship carried several thousand troops who were being rotated back to the States for discharge or further assignment. I really can't remember how we were all sorted out and eventually assigned to our respective places. Pity those in charge!

For those of you who have never traveled on a troop transport, I need to describe our quarters. Troop transports are not built for pleasure but to provide the best way to transport by sea the maximum number of people (usually troops) to any designated place. So, individual staterooms are not provided. Instead, bunks, made of canvas laced to steel pipe frames, are attached to bulkheads (walls) or steel pillars, and piled four- or five-high in each hold. The holds are designated by letters of the alphabet, with "A" hold being nearest the top deck. There are not many decks, as with a cruise liner, just the top deck for a walking surface. Mess halls and kitchens are below decks. No sitting at a table for six, with linen tablecloths and flowers, and waiters to hand you the menu. You stand in line for your food, sit down to eat at narrow tables which, with their narrow benches, are secured to the deck. Your knees probably knock against those of your neighbor across from you. After eating, you "bus" your own tray and move on out so the next group can come in for their meal.

Women and girls were assigned to the forward holds, and men and boys to the holds toward the stern. Mother, Ruth, and I were sent to "C" hold, the third one down. I believe there was one hold even lower than ours, but we were pretty near the bottom of the ship. There was room between the bunks to sit hunched over, if you weren't too big. You could turn over without bumping the person above you, but you couldn't sit straight up.

Narrow aisles went between the tiers of bunks, and the entire hold was filled with the tiers. Entry from above was by steel ladder steps, quite narrow, and very steep. There were several such ladders for each hold, to expedite getting to meals, or for evacuation, should that be necessary. A few suitcases or such could be stored under the bottom bunk, but otherwise there was no storage space. We kept our few clothes rolled up in our bunks. Good thing that we internees had so few material possessions. I don't know where we could have stowed them! As it was, a number of women had collected some cosmetics, and they stashed them on the I-beams that formed the support for the deck above. Not a very secure storage space, as we would find out!

Our bathrooms, well, really toilets, and called "heads" in Navy terms, were at the bow of the ship—not too bad in good weather, pretty awful in rough weather. Interestingly enough to those of us from Los Baños, the latrines were made much the same way ours in Camp had been made. A long stainless steel trough, with water running constantly through it (that was an improvement over Camp!), and many holes positioned above the trough served our physical needs. Hang the aesthetics! At least they provided toilet paper, which had been a luxury, if even available, when we were at Los Baños. The problem came in really rough weather when sometimes the bow was up, away up, and in the next moment was abruptly pitched down. That did wondrous things to the flow of water and other contents!

Across the Pacific

On April 13, 1945 (it was April 12 in the States), we were at anchor just off Tacloban, Leyte, where our troops had made their first Philippine landing. We were waiting for the arrival of our escort ships which were supposed to be with us on our trip east across the Pacific. While there, we heard the news of the death of President F. D. Roosevelt. Within the next day or two, we were joined by two destroyer escorts and started on our journey. By this time, we were seasoned "troopers." We younger ones could scamper up and down the gangways (ladders) as fast as any sailor. Our voyage was to take about three weeks, so we got lots of practice.

Since this was a military ship, military police were part of the crew, and they patrolled the ship, including the holds, on a 24-hour basis. We never knew when they would be coming through, and sometimes we were rather skimpily dressed. Ventilation was sometimes not the best in the lower holds, and many women slept in the bare minimum. I remember waking up one night when the woman in the top bunk in the tier opposite mine raised up on one elbow and said to the M.P. who was standing on the gangway, his dimmed flashlight shining on her, "Enjoying the view, buddy?" He moved on quickly.

Tacloban was perhaps a week behind us when we ran into one of the worst storms at sea I have ever experienced. This was my fifth Pacific Ocean crossing, and we almost always had a storm or two en route on previous trips. During the first day or two of the typhoon, we were fortunate to be heading into the storm, so we simply pitched up and down. The waves were huge and no one could be on deck. The second night, as we were sleeping, or trying to sleep, the ship was suddenly turned 90 degrees to our former course. That put us in the trough, with the waves pushing us to one side and then another. I don't know how many degrees roll we took, back and forth several times. Each time we would come up ever so slowly. I was sure that we were going to turn completely over. Any loose stuff, of course, was thrown every which way. It was especially bad when the cosmetics flew off the I-beams and became missles or else broke into pieces when they hit the deck (steel, not wood). The hold stank of perfume.

Even worse was the pandemonium of frightened, sea-sick women. It was a mess! But, yet again, our Lord graciously kept ship and passengers safe, and gradually we came about once more on course, pitching up and down, but not rolling. We heard the next morning that our Captain had had to turn the 90 degrees to avoid colliding with a blacked out U.S. ship convoy which was cutting across our path. Radar was not very effective with the waves being so high. If a ship were down in a trough, the radar would simply go over her. Of course, all ships were traveling in a blacked out condition, and the typhoon was raging. Our escort ships had been unable to keep up with us in the storm, and we saw them no more as we continued our solitary way eastward toward the States.

Home At Last

Finally, we reached our destination, San Pedro, port of Los Angeles on May 2, 1945. We had actually come into the harbor during the night before but debarked the next day. We were met by the Red Cross, and Army trucks were there to take us to a large hall (Elks Club) in Los Angeles, where our relatives were anxiously awaiting us. There we would be processed and sent on our various ways. Fortunately for us, our families lived in nearby Pasadena, so we didn't have too far to go. But, it was late at night before all the red tape was finished and we could leave. Grandpa Wilson was there. Mother's brother, Kenneth, and his family also came to meet us. Grandpa's letter to his other daughters tells of his dismay at the condition of Dad and Mother. He calls them "<u>thin</u> and <u>haggard</u>, hollow eyed and weak . . ." (underlining, his). He was aghast at our lack of decent clothing, especially underwear! But, he also notes that we were in good spirits and "giving thanks to God for their timely rescue and safe voyage home."

We celebrated Dad and Mother's twenty-seventh wedding anniversary the day after our arrival in the States, May 3, 1945. Uncle Albert and Aunt Florence graciously let us live in their home until we could locate a home of our own. Then we settled down to regain health and strength and start gathering together necessary furniture and clothing for the family. Many people generously gave material things of all sorts, and before long we were comfortably living in our own home in Pasadena, California.

PART THREE

EPILOGUE

For months after our return from the Philippines, we frequently were asked to appear before church audiences and speak of our experiences. Dad and Mother did the main presentations, but we three younger kids were expected to appear on the platform also and perhaps speak briefly or answer questions from the young people. Though the folks spoke of mission work in the Philippines, most often people wanted to hear of our war experiences. The most frequently asked question was, "Do you hate the Japanese?" Our unanimous answer was always, "NO, we don't hate them. Their actions were often hateful and cruel, but we prayed for them as for any human being. Jesus died for ALL people, also for our enemies. Of course, we also prayed to be delivered from our captivity, if it was God's will." Most of our Japanese guards had been killed in the daring raid that rescued us, but Lt. Konishi, our nemesis, had escaped in the confusion. A few months later, around July 1945, Konishi, working as a golf caddy, had been recognized by a former internee. He was arrested, tried as a war criminal, and executed in 1947.

For us young people, school soon took up most of our time. All of us who had received our schooling under severely trying circumstances were able to pass the achievement tests and enter our proper grade levels when we came back to the States. For me that meant summer school in 1945, where one of my teachers was the same Miss Judson who had been interned and then repatriated. Then, in September of 1945, I entered my senior year of high school at Pasadena Junior College, which had the last two years of high school and the first two years of college at the same campus. David entered a junior high school, and Ruth went off to take her first year of college at Wheaton, Illinois. Mother and Dad were grappling with the everyday matters of starting life all

149

over again!

Early in 1946 Dad went back to the Philippines to help with the post-war rebuilding program; Mother stayed on to keep the family together. That fall, Ruth and I were both at Pasadena City College, both in pre-nursing courses. Being "twice shy" after being "once burned" in romantic affairs, I hadn't dated at all as a high school senior. Even into my first year of college, I kept busy with school and church affairs, and never single dated. My plans were to complete college, earn my nursing degree, and apply to a foreign mission board.

But, I had a girl friend (Jean McMurdie) whose elder brother, Bill, home from the war in Europe, told her to "find me a suitable wife." She took the oblique path and maneuvered Bill into accepting a college Red Cross division chairmanship where he was my "boss." So, he and I got to know each other in a very natural way. Bill was a tall (6'4"), red-headed, and blue-eyed young man who was taking college engineering classes. Yes! I was interested! My youthful intention to never marry a blue-eyed, red-headed man (where do kids get these fancies?) seemed not so important now. The only thing I really didn't want to do was to marry a preacher! Definitely not! But, Bill was energetically pursuing his engineering studies and that seemed a good career choice. There was just one problem: he didn't seem to notice me much, all that fall semester of 1946.

One afternoon in March of 1947, we were both working late on a Red Cross project when Bill diffidently asked if I would like to go to his house for supper instead of taking the long bus ride home. He brought me into the house through the back door and into the kitchen, much to the scandalized dismay of his grandmother, who was getting supper. But, his family was very cordial and, of course, I already knew Jean.

Things progressed. My Latin teacher was disappointed in my nose-diving grades (I never got below a B-, but I had been carrying a straight A in the course.) My friends noticed that I was preoccupied. Bill and I were sitting in his dad's car in front of my house when he proposed and I accepted. THEN he said, "I think I'd better tell you that I've changed my major, and I will be attending seminary to prepare to be a preacher." I was totally shocked! But, when he offered to let me have a week to reconsider, somehow I knew that this man was my life partner and told him the proposal and acceptance stood. So, now

I was committed to a red-haired, blue-eyed, future preacher! That was May 1947.

We were married in August of 1947 and moved east to Springfield, Illinois. Joining the incoming freshman class at Concordia Seminary, we found we were among a large group of former service men and their wives. This influx of more mature, war-weary men changed the face of the campus for several years in a row.

Neither Bill nor any of the other former G.I.'s ever talked much about their war experiences. They were too recent and too painful. Once we were amazed and concerned to see one of the student wives at church with a split lip and other facial contusions. She and her husband were both rather small people, he being about welter-weight size. We said, jokingly, "What happened, Helen? Did Leo hit you?" Her eyes twinkled as she assented, and the embarrassed Leo told us that sometimes he had nightmares about his war experiences, and would strike out with his arms trying to protect himself. It was comforting to have fellow students who understood the problem.

In the five years we were at seminary, my family spread all over the world. Brother Allen and his wife were missionaries in Iran, where he had been stationed during the war. Brother Bill was busy helping with the construction of the Grand Coulee Dam in Washington state. He and his wife had three kids. Ruth had completed her bachelor's degree in nursing and was working in mission hospitals in the Philippines, where she met a missionary whom she would marry in 1953. Brother Dave, having served a term in the Navy, had married and was in college in California. Dad and Mother were well into their first post-war term of service under the national church in the Philippines.

After two childless years, Bill and I decided that it would be good to apply for admission to a hospital school of nursing. But, in 1949 very few schools of nursing accepted married students. However, with my scholastic background, said the dean, they would be happy to have me as a student. But, I would have to abide by their house rules, one of which was that all students must live in the dorm and would have privileges to have visitors once a week on Wednesday afternoons! I politely declined the offer.

The good Lord brought us our family the "hard" way. After long years of yearning for children, we were able to adopt two. John, our son, came to us during Bill's last year at the seminary. The adoptions officer, bless her heart, ignored the fact Bill's G.I. bill subsidy had run out and that we were barely supporting ourselves. Six months later, Bill would be settled in his first parish, where income, though small, was more than adequate. After another year or two, our daughter Mary came to live with us, and our family was complete.

So, much more could be said. After all, the war years, which seem to evoke the most interest, took up only a little more than three years of my life. My *Epilogue* takes up fifty-five more years! Did I ever achieve my goal of becoming a nurse? Was my health affected by my war-time years? Did I ever get back to visit my childhood home?

YES! to all the above!

Achieve my goal to be a nurse? After working seven years as a Licensed Practical Nurse, I entered the four-year baccalaureate course at Pacific Lutheran University. I received my bachelor's degree in nursing in 1976. Most of my classmates were my kids' ages, and I was older than several of my professors. Passing the State Boards, I gained my cherished Registered Nurse license. I've worked in hospitals, community health, and prisons. (When I worked at the prison, Bill loved telling people that I'd just gotten out of jail!)

Health? Nutritional deprivation during the war seems to have affected my muscles and joints to some extent through the years, but for the most part I keep going without too much trouble. My eyes recovered from the starvation stress, and with new eyeglasses, I've no problems.

Get back home? In 1988, sister Ruth and I made our "balikbayan," or homecoming, trip to our old home (the Richmond house) in Albay, which had survived unscathed in the violent battle to retake Legaspi; to Manila, where we located Ellinwood Dormitory and our old rooms; and to Los Baños, where we found only a modest bronze plaque commemorating the Los Baños Internment Camp. All the thatch buildings were long gone. Jungle had reclaimed the area where our barracks once stood. With full hearts we looked over to the grounds where the amtracs, on that not-to-be-forgotten February day, had arrived to take on their loads of precious human cargo.

TO GOD ALONE BE GLORY!
"His eye is on the sparrow, And I know He watches me!"

Plaque at Los Baños, June 1988

Five Los Baños Internment Camp Survivors, January 2001
L to R: George MacDonald, Ruth McAnlis Haney, David McAnlis,
Jean McAnlis McMurdie, Tom Bousman

ORDER FORM

Jean McMurdie
2311-B Via Puerta
Laguna Woods, CA 92653
mjmcmurdie@aol.com

Date_____

SHIP TO			

DESCRIPTION	QTY	PRICE	AMOUNT
LAND OF THE MORNING *A Civilian Internee's Poignant Memories* *of Sunshine and Shadows* Jean McAnlis McMurdie ISBN 1-880222-43-4		$14.95	
Washington residents 8% tax			
Price includes shipping & handling			
	TOTAL		